THE
Archive Photographs
SERIES

BURTON UPON TRENT
TALES OF THE TOWN

A wonderfully evocative photograph of the Burton that is lost and gone forever. Once this was a typical view all around the town, a normal part of the everyday scene still recalled by many people, possibly in retrospect, with nostalgia. The picture is so atmospheric that one can almost feel the chill of this cold, misty winter day and smell the smoke and the steam and the aromas of brewing and malting, accompanied by the sounds of the engine, the clanking of the wagons and, perhaps, in the background, the hammering of coopers at work or of brewery machinery. We wait for the clang as the signal arm drops, allowing the train to move slowly forward over one of those many level crossings that we once cursed and grumbled about. The picture chose itself to be the frontispiece for our book about times past. The scene was located within the extensive area of the Bass Middle Brewery situated between Station Street and Guild Street. The semaphore signal replaced an old original cross-bar signal. The building behind the ground frame levers was the Fire Office; on the right was the Ale and Hop Store. Number 2 Union Room lies ahead and there are loading banks alongside the rail tracks.

THE
Archive Photographs
SERIES

BURTON UPON TRENT
TALES OF THE TOWN

Compiled by
Geoffrey Sowerby and Richard Farman

'I perceive this to be Old Burton', the Rat remarked approvingly, 'Sensible Mole!
The very thing.' (The Wind In The Willows, *Kenneth Grahame*)

CHALFORD

First published 1997
Copyright © Geoffrey Sowerby and Richard Farman 1997

The Chalford Publishing Company
St Mary's Mill, Chalford,
Stroud, Gloucestershire, GL6 8NX

ISBN 0 7524 1097 0

Typesetting and origination by
The Chalford Publishing Company
Printed in Great Britain by
Bailey Print, Dursley, Gloucestershire

'When the student at Oxford was asked what man had most benefited humanity and when he answered "Bass", I think that he should not have been plucked. It was a fair average answer.' (Rachel Ray, Anthony Trollope, 1863)

Postcard-piracy and touching-up have been used for this amusing little cameo. In its original form this was a French *carte postale* with the simple message 'C'*est bon*' and an old French couple plainly enjoying a glass of red wine, in spite of a superimposed advertisement for Bass's No. 1. In this later reprint a wine carafe has been blacked out, the French inscription removed and an unlikely label attached to the wine bottle.

Contents

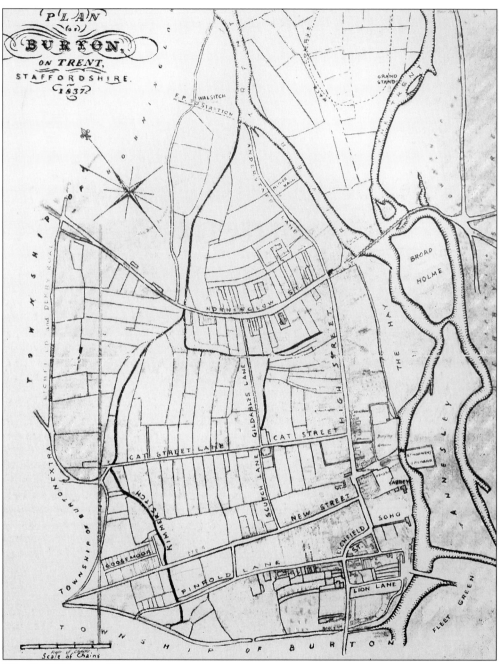

Wood's 1837 map of Burton.

One
Setting the Scenes

The good citizens of Burton upon Trent, asleep in their beds in the early hours of 20 June 1837, would be unaware that a great new era was just beginning.

Shortly after 2.00 am Dr Howley the Archbishop of Canterbury, and the Marquess of Conyngham the Lord Chancellor, hurriedly left Windsor Castle for London. People along the rough, bumpy road may have stirred in their sleep and wondered at the cause of the unusual galloping of horses and rattling of flying wheels as these gentlemen sped past. It took nearly three hours to reach Kensington Palace and they then faced the problem of arousing slumbering servants and convincing them of the urgency of their mission. Their task was to inform the young Princess Victoria, just eighteen years of age, that her uncle, King William IV, was dead and that she was now Queen of England. She was destined to reign for nearly sixty-four years and to give her name to the momentous period in world history - and in the story of Burton upon Trent - which we now designate as the Victorian era.

Of course the pattern of history, development and change cannot be pin-pointed to a single event or to one particular year. The foundations of the Victorian age were laid prior to 1837 but it seemed, nevertheless, both a significant and convenient point from which to commence this anthology of Burton upon Trent events and personalities.

Significantly, there was Wood's map of Burton published in 1837, one of the first detailed plans of the town allowing us to look down on its features and extent at that time. On 12 November 1837 Michael Arthur Bass was born in the family's town house at 136 High Street. It is not inappropriate that he should have arrived on the scene in the year of Queen Victoria's accession since, as Lord Burton, he epitomises the industrial barons of the nineteenth century who made such notable contributions to Victorian life and times, both nationally and locally. Among those present at the young Queen's first Council was the Marquess of Anglesey, ground landlord of much of Burton upon Trent, whose successors were to continue to figure in the story of the town.

Immediately following Victoria's accession there were other highly significant events encouraging the commercial growth of Burton, among them the establishment of railway communication in 1839 and the opening of the Burton Union Bank on 11 October the same year. Also of great importance was the advent of the penny post in 1840. It is worth recording too, that these years saw the coming of photographic processes by Daguerre and Fox Talbot, eventually enabling many local scenes and events to be recorded for posterity and their subsequent reproduction to help illustrate these tales of the town.

The general development, layout and character of Burton as largely established in Victorian times remained comparatively unaltered until after the Second World War, when many sweeping changes began to take place. It seemed reasonable therefore, to set this particular volume within the broad framework of the period 1837-1939, but we decided to add a brief reminder of the early war years. So while a round figure might have been logical, we are pleased to offer, as modern advertising might have it, a few extra years for the price of a hundred.

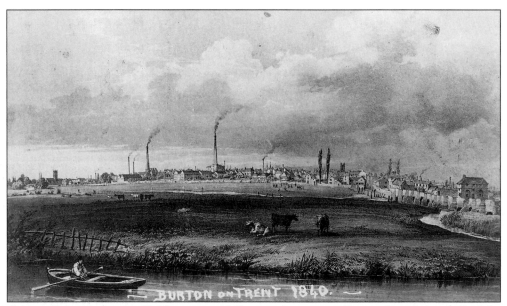

A print from a picture by K. Thomas, c. 1840, provides an overall view from Stapenhill of the town between the Parish Church (left) and the old bridge, well portrayed, right. The earliest brewery chimneys are already beginning to create the distinctive sky line which dominated later views. The original Holy Trinity Church of 1824 (half right) has a tower, which was replaced by a spire when rebuilt in 1880-82.

The Bass town house decorated for the Coronation of King Edward VII in August 1902. The whole of Bass's High Street frontage was elaborately dressed and this doorway honoured Queen Alexandra. The lights came on every evening and Burtonians paraded up and down admiring the spectacle. It was a little unfortunate that roof repairs were in progress at the time.

In spite of its poor condition this is one of the most striking early photographs of the original Great Bridge of Burton, which served the town from at least the twelfth century until its removal after the new bridge was opened on 22 June 1864. This view emphasises how the early structure ran within the line of the river, reducing pressure on the arches, and then curved round towards the foot of Bearwood Hill (just discernible, centre). Its narrowness and the considerable traffic it carried demanded frequent refuges each side. The building (left) survives in Meadow Lane, its adjoining premises becoming Boddington's brewery, then, for a time, Everards, before it was established as the Swan Works of C.J. Spooner, the wood carver. He eventually joined with Ortons of Princess Street in Victoria Crescent (1934). The yard (left) was that of William Clarke, stonemason.

William Wyatt's survey of Stapenhill (1757) shows the old road to the village running off Ashby Road along the foothills of Scalpcliff before descending near the present Elms Inn; it also marks the projected 'new turnpike road', establishing today's Stapenhill Road. This portion of a panoramic Burton view of around 1860 includes, on the extreme right, the toll house and gate for the Burton-Measham road, turnpiked in 1763. The development of railways ended the coaching era and started the rapid decline of turnpike trusts from 1,100 in the 1860s to two by 1890.

Dating back to medieval times an annual horse fair was held in Horninglow Street on 20 October, until 1924. The scene is captured in a painting dated 1903 by S. Garratt, which is now in Burton Library. The public house (left) was the Rising Sun. Change was soon to come when tram lines were laid and subsequently this part of one of Burton's oldest streets was much altered. Holy Trinity Church was demolished in 1973 and other properties were swept away during redevelopment. The foundation stone of the first church was laid in 1824 by Revd Thomas Gisborne on behalf of the first Marquess of Anglesey, although an engraved copper plate recorded the name of the Marquess. The foundation stone of the second church was laid in 1880 by the fourth Marquess of Anglesey.

Opposite: This area, known as the Soho, is now completely occupied by the Technical College. These buildings were originally warehouses with wharves, dating from when the Trent was made navigable to this point in the early eighteenth century, making Bond End a busy trading and manufacturing locality. Later converted to residences, they remained until after the Second World War. The present Abbey Inn can be seen along the bank but changes to the river courses are apparent in this view from the Ferry Bridge.

Some superior buildings were beginning to appear along Station Street, one such being the first Baptist Chapel of 1803. The costumes help to date this steel engraving to well before 1861 when fire destroyed the building. Its successor lasted until the present chapel was built in 1957.

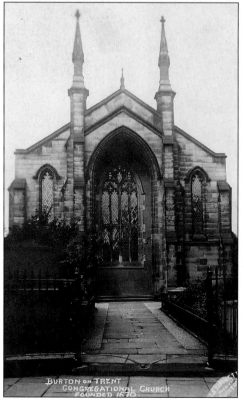

The map on page 6 shows the location of Burton's old racecourse (top right) and, alongside near the river, the grandstand. When that was taken down in 1840, stone from it was used to build the porch of the Congregational Church in High Street (1842). They were the first Nonconformist body to become established in Burton over 300 years ago. This particular card is marked as a souvenir of 'Mother and Dad's wedding' on Easter Monday 28 March 1910.

Two
'Each Night to the Play'

This Edwardian High Street photograph of Worthington's crossing is fairly familiar, but virtually unknown is the historic significance of the old Blue Posts seen beyond the crossing. It was demolished in 1927 and replaced by the present inn. During the early nineteenth century it was occupied by the Yeomans family who had a small brewery adjoining. In the late 1830s an original piece of doggerel verse was spoken (and probably written) by a Mr Thorne as a prologue for a theatrical performance. Its nineteen verses describe visiting thirty-four public houses, sampling the ale at each, and providing a valuable list of town centre inns and beer houses of the period. Its last verse then reveals the elusive location of what was almost certainly Burton's earliest 'theatre'.

Mr Thorne's Poem

Your servant, kind gentlefolks, whom to address
It's a pleasure I cannot find words to express;
For to Burton I am come, and of all other places
You are sure to meet there honest hearts and kind faces.

Of the famed Burton ale I have oft heard folks pother,
Which in goodness and flavour surpasses all other;
So grant me your patience, I'll not keep you long,
But an opinion I'll give of each house in a song.

At the famous **Bear Inn**, as you come into town,
If you'll take a good glass you may sit yourself down;
There's a house too, hard by, where you'll fare quite as well,
If you only just ring at the sign of the **Bell**.

And when at the **Bell** you have made yourself mellow,
At the **Roebuck** you'll meet with a good jovial fellow,
But you must not stay long or I'll wager a crown,
That his ale or his hammer will soon fetch you down.

Distilled from the juice of the grape is good wine,
And good malt liquor distilled at the **Vine**,
And if, sailor-like, you love grog and good flip,
You'll find a snug cabin enough at the **Ship**.

Having called at the **Talbot**, it surely won't fail,
The **Swan**, too, you'll find, swims in very good ale,
And when at the next house you've drinking begun,
You'll scarce tell which shines brightest, your face or the **Sun**.

A hungry man need not be thought such a glutton
Should he stop when he meets with a **Shoulder of Mutton**;
Though the meat, you'll soon find, is not, like the ale, good -
For the ale's made from malt, and the mutton from wood.

At the **Saracen's Head** you'll meet with good ale,
May never the liquor or customers fail,
But if humour for keeping good company leans
You'll get drunk as a lord with the famous **Three Queens**.

To mix mirth with good ale, if your fancy incline,
There's a house just by, but I'll not name the sign;
But I'll wager if once you to tippling give loose,
Though as sly as a **Fox**, you'll walk out like a **Goose**.

To the old **Coach And Horses** if once you but drive,
The landlord and liquor will keep you alive;
But if, o'er your liquor, should drowsiness creep,
At the sign of the **Lamb** you'll kill time like a sheep.

Having called at the **Boot**, you can scarcely fare worse,
But just taste a glass at the famous **White Horse.**
You'll find it surpasses all mortal belief -
There's often good barley found in a **Wheatsheaf**.

The fare at the **White Hart's** unequalled, you'll own;
But do not neglect first to call at the **Crown**,
Where the landlord will make you both happy and easy,
For his house and his heart are both open to please ye.

At the old **Angel Inn**, and the famous **White Lion**,
Their very best ale you may surely rely on;
There's a house, too, hard by, where you may drink of a flagon,
Till, as bold as **St George**, you may fight with a **Dragon**.

From the **Dog** you may sail to the old **Anchor Inn**,
And having cast anchor, may drinking begin;
Should home for the best sometimes lose its charms,
You'll meet mirth in high glee at the **Carpenter's Arms**.

On **Prussia's** famed **King** you may call if you please,
The Nag's Head from thence you will soon cross with ease;
Having drunk at the **Lion**, you'll hardly be dry,
But you must not attempt from the **Eagle** to fly.

To drink punch at the **Punch Bowl** you'll feel sure inclined,
There's a house near the church, I forgot, you'll soon find,
Having tasted the ale, you'll acknowledge ere soon,
On such ale you could live like the **Man-in-The-Moon**.

Having turned yourself round, you see a large **Oak**
Which made England to smile, and other nations to smoke;
The leaves of the tree, you may see, are some use,
And the butt of the tree contains barley juice.

Where pain and misfortune in wretchedness pined,
From a prison converted, an inn you will find,
Where once his hard fortune each man did bewail
He now laughs, sings and smokes o'er his pitcher of ale.

But hold, don't forget, pray, to call at the **Star**,
The famed ale of which must have reached you afar.
Then banish life's crosses, cross over the way,
And pass through the **BLUE POSTS** each night to the PLAY.

The Three Queens visited in the poem is the present Queens' Hotel, formerly one of the town's principal posting houses. This is a later reproduction, as acknowledged, of earlier hotel stationery. Burton's oldest inn, the original building is recorded as being licensed in 1531. The ladies claimed as visitors were Mary Queen of Scots, Queen Elizabeth and Queen Adelaide, consort of King William IV.

One old Burton inn mentioned in Mr Thorne's poem, the Vine, closed shortly afterwards, *c.* 1840. It then became Holy Trinity Vicarage (175 Horninglow Street), used as such until the 1950s. The Vine had been a coaching inn and its entrance archway and rear yard are seen here. One wonders about the contrasting uses of the room now indicated here as the vicar's study. This 1907 mothers' meeting depicts a fine Edwardian fashion display with the vicar, Revd H.T. Boultbee, unassumingly tucked away in his deck chair (left). He could never have imagined that his church site would become a super store and that his vicarage would give way to a garage.

Another old inn mentioned in the poem was The Man In The Moon in the Market Place (left). It had balconies making it a vantage point for viewing public events and processions to the Parish Church. Here, dignitaries are arriving for the memorial service for King Edward VII in 1910. Everything in this view has gone, the shopping precinct now replacing Bank Square which included another of Mr Thorne's inns, inspiring the great rhyme: '...The White Lion, Their very best ale you can surely rely on.'

Three

An Artist's Last Pictures

Members of the Clay family became noted figures in the story of Burton from the eighteenth to the twentieth century. From the time Joseph Clay came to the Lamb and Flag inn in Horninglow Street, they featured prominently in the brewing industry. In 1792 Joseph built the fine house, No. 5 Horninglow Street (below) on the site of the Lamb and Flag. It is now named Clay House.

Joseph's son, Joseph Clay II, became a banker as well as a brewer and was the first of the family to live at Stapenhill House. Joseph II's younger sons, Joseph III and John became clergymen. In 1833 these two brothers and their sister founded St John's Church at Newhall, which had previously been part of the parish of Stapenhill. Revd Joseph died in 1839 but Revd John Clay was Vicar of Stapenhill from 1835 until 1875. In 1843 he married Jessie, daughter of John Harden of Brathay Hall near Ambleside.

Although not a professional artist, John Harden was a painter of considerable ability with an extensive and wide ranging output of pictures to his credit. At the time of Jessie's marriage he was over seventy but still drawing and painting. Between 1844 and 1847 he paid visits to the Clays at Stapenhill Vicarage and produced watercolours and drawings of local scenes, mainly of Stapenhill. These paintings are among his last works and some are felt not to be of quite the high standard of earlier pictures which were not, of course, of this area. Nevertheless they are of great interest as impressions of scenes from a period from which photographs are lacking, so we are pleased to be able to include examples of his Stapenhill views and accord him wider local recognition. John Harden spent the months from September 1846 to April 1847 in Stapenhill and recorded that it was a very severe winter with heavy snow and bitter winds until the early part of April. He died in July 1847, shortly after returning home. Later, Revd Clay and Jessie retired to the Lake District and they too are buried in Brathay churchyard.

John Harding called this painting *The Triangle, Stapenhill*, a slightly unromantic title for a picture given rather romantic treatment, with leisurely villagers chatting together on the old village green. There is also some artistic licence in giving St Peter's Street a gradient, no doubt to raise the background with the row of cottages behind the central tree shown with three storeys. They remain, in fact, outwardly little altered today from how they actually were in the 1840s. One of them had been a small beer house called The North Pole. The present owners have perpetuated and displayed this splendid name from times long past.

The ancient trees painted by John Harden just lasted into the new century when they were becoming both unsightly and dangerous. Looking at this photograph, cutting them down and removing their long-established roots was obviously a laborious manual task. The Clay's vicarage with its out buildings forms the background. A new vicarage had been built opposite the church and the old house was now the residence of the Samble family. It was demolished in the mid-1930s along with Stapenhill House when the Pleasure Gardens were laid out.

John Harden shows the other side of Stapenhill Green - soon to be occupied by shops and school (now the Bridge Surgery) - as a picturesque group of buildings, although the realism of the camera may have disillusioned us. He entitled this picture *The Gate of the Revd John Clay* - this being the archway seen in the vicarage garden wall where traffic now pours on to St Peter's Bridge. Main Street drops down to the left, the wall continuing to join that around Stapenhill House.

There is certainly nothing idyllic about this photographic view of the green, seen from Stapenhill Road, with all of John Harden's rustic scene swept away (except for the former vicarage, right). Today's trees, newly planted to replace the old ones on a levelled 'triangle', are established within metal frames but although benches have been provided, there are no villagers chatting in the shadow of the new tram/lamp standard. We can date Simnett's picture to after 1906 as all Burton's trams were open top until then, when most were give top deck covers. The house numbered 1 Main Street (facing the camera) was demolished around 1970 but the shops still remain in use after housing a variety of businesses. The one visible behind the tram was, at this time, an Ind Coope wines and spirits shop. During the First World War the premises were used by Mrs Lily Thomas as her collecting point for parcels to be dispatched to prisoners of war.

John Harden's *Stapenhill Village* scene was painted from near the foot of Hill Street looking towards the Barley Mow. Little else is recognisable now and the old church of his day seems to have acquired rather majestic proportions. It is again a reminder of how the work of an artist has to be viewed with reservations as to how far it represents a true pictorial record.

One wonders if this photograph, *c.* 1900, was carefully posed with the servant girl watching the milkman fill her jug from his pail. He is believed to be Mr Brooks of Hill Street. Again we see the Barley Mow and, beyond, the old Punch Bowl and the church tower. The Co-op shop has not yet appeared on Ferry Street corner which was soon to become the tram terminus; perhaps the most striking impression here is of the traffic-free serenity, not to last much longer.

Four
Edward Meets Mr Bass

Edward Glover was no doubt a rather nervous young man when, on 1 April 1848, accompanied by his widowed mother Sarah, he was ushered into the presence of Michael Thomas Bass, his brother Abraham Bass, an attorney and John Richardson, the town's high bailiff and coroner. These gentlemen had gathered as Managers of the Burton upon Trent British School in Guidables Lane (later Guild Street), built 1843-4. They were to witness the signing of an indenture binding Edward for four years as apprentice to James Samble, master of the school.

In 1803 British Schools were started by the Nonconformists to provide elementary education for children, the Church of England National Schools following suit. The earliest local foundations (around 1827) were Horninglow Street (later Hawkins Lane), Anderstaff and Christ Church. Under a pupil-teacher system evolved in 1846, schools receiving a favourable report from inspectors were recognised for the training and employment of stipendiary monitors from thirteen plus. They were paid £10 in the first year with annual increments to reach £20 after completing apprenticeship. If successful they could take additional training to be paid as minor civil servants.

The government now contributed £15 to £20, with the Managers giving twice that sum, provided that the Inspectorate approved the school's efficiency. After two years the grant might be £20 to £25, and £25 to £30 after three years, so James Samble was probably receiving less than £100 per annum for his services. For training Edward as a pupil-teacher he was paid an extra £5 a year. As was often the case his post carried with it a school house while his wife, Elizabeth, was the school mistress, looking after the younger children and the girls. Mistresses, however, were only paid two-thirds of the going rates.

Now we can go back to young Edward, anxiously listening as the provisions of his indenture were read out, explained and then duly signed by all present. Serving James Samble for four years 'in the business of a school master' Edward agreed that 'he shall not, except from illness, absent himself from the said school during school hours and shall conduct himself with honesty, sobriety and temperance, and not be guilty of lewd or profane conversation, conduct, or of gambling or any immorality, but shall diligently and obediently assist in the instruction and discipline of the scholars under the direction of the master, and apply himself with industry to the instructions which shall be given to him... and shall regularly attend divine service on Sunday.' Edward's mother undertook to provide all proper lodging, food, apparel, washing, medicine and medical attendance.

James Samble undertook (for his extra £5 per annum) 'to the best of his ability to teach the business of a schoolmaster... and afford daily opportunities (Sunday and the usual school holidays only excepted) of observing and practising the art of teaching... and to devote one hour and a half at the least in every morning or evening, before or after the usual hours of school - keeping to the further personal instruction... in the several branches of useful learning taught in the said school.'

This 'useful learning' was elaborated. After year one Edward had to read with fluency, ease and expression; write neatly with correct spelling and punctuation; write from dictation sums in the first four compound rules of arithmetic and know the tables of weights and measures; and point out the parts of speech in a simple sentence and give the rules of its construction. He must have an elementary knowledge of geography and satisfactory religious knowledge, with the first rudiments in schools where vocal music was taught. In years two and three there was progression in each category - arithmetic, grammar, writing, reading, geography - year two, for example, requiring knowledge of the geography of Great Britain and Palestine. Europe was not added until year three!

So to the vital examination at the end of year four: 1. To prepare an oral lesson with notes on a subject chosen by the Inspector; 2. To work sums in decimal arithmetic and show acquaintance with the rules of mental arithmetic; 3. In grammar to be examined in etymology; 4. To know the geography of the four quarters of the world and especially of the British Empire; 5. To know a general outline of English history; 6. To examine a class and give an oral lesson keeping the class attentive, in order, and in activity, without undue noise. As in each previous year he was required to be clean in person and dress and to present a Certificate of Good Conduct from the Managers and one of Punctuality, Diligence, Obedience and Attention to Duties from the Master. Girl pupil-teachers were required to show increasing skills as sempstresses and as teachers of sewing, knitting etc.

Thus began Edward's chosen career. Unfortunately no records have come to light to reveal his subsequent progress but his immaculately preserved indenture allows us to recreate this local scene of 150 years ago.

Pupil-teacher training had continued in the town but in 1907 Burton Education Committee opened Wellington Street school as a pupil-teacher centre. These students participate in an end-of-session play performance following the 1908 examinations, commented on as follows: 'What do you think of Prelim. Result? I am glad that I have obtained a distinction in a compulsory subject. Both my others were in optionals. No one here out of forty has more than two distinctions.' The figure of forty shows the extent to which the scheme operated but by 1914 it was no longer favoured by the government and the centre closed.

While Edward Glover was being interviewed for the British School, Stretton children were being taught in their new National School, on which a foundation stone recorded the year 1842 and named the Marquess of Anglesey. Miss Sarah Cope was the first mistress. Though long since demolished it remained, as seen here, after a new school was built but the whole site is now being redeveloped. Stretton Church was also a small brick building costing £900, erected at the same time as the school. It was replaced by St Mary's Church in 1897, a £30,000 gift from Mr J. Gretton.

In the chair for Edward Glover's interview was Michael Thomas Bass (1799-1884), head of the rapidly expanding brewery business. He became Liberal MP for Derby in 1848 and was a noted benefactor both there and in Burton. After building and endowing St Paul's Church in 1874, he also built St Margaret's in Shobnall Street in 1881 as a chapel-of-ease to St Paul's.

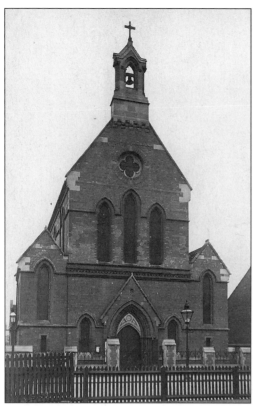

Photographs of St Margaret's Church are fairly scarce but here are both exterior and interior views. St Margaret's catered for an additional 600 sittings and its construction shortly after St Paul's was opened reflected the extensive residential growth of this part of Burton and the need for Sunday School accommodation. After demolition in 1970 the site was developed as Shobnall Close. St Margaret's House, which adjoined, had been used by the Sisters of Bethany when they worked in the parish.

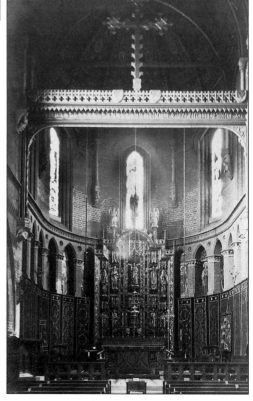

Some features from the interior of St Margaret's can still be discovered in St Paul's, notably a mural in honour of the benefactor, the lectern, the altar and the figure of St Margaret. The decorative gilt reredos found a home in Shropshire at the church of Priorslee near Oakengates.

Following the Education Act of 1870 the Burton School Board was established and the first new school built was Victoria Road, which opened on 27 May 1875. This photograph of the boys' department was certainly taken quite early on in the school's long history with best clothes the order of the day. Note the wide range of smart neckwear - lace, sailor and stiff collars, ordinary ties and bow ties. The background room became a science laboratory when Victoria Road became a senior school. Its benches remained, at first posing problems when it reverted again to being a junior school. Lines of low desks between the benches left only rows of heads visible from the dais. Remaining quite unchanged was the white tiled public toilet type doorway out of the playground.

Some true little gems from Victoria Road School.
'Dear Sir, I am not going to let J—— go to the baths until she can swim.'
'Babby Jesus was rapped up in Swadlincoat.'
'Sir. I am sorry P—— has been away but we all had trouble with our bowels at the same time.'

A few years after Edward Glover embarked on his teaching career, another young man signed his indenture of apprenticeship to be 'taught and instructed in the art of a surgeon and apothecary.' Arthur Nadin, aged 17, was the son of Joseph Nadin, coalmaster of Stapenhill. On 5 January 1852 Arthur was bound for five years to Robert Tomlinson and George Lowe, surgeons and apothecaries, 'in consideration of the sum of one hundred and ninety-nine pounds sterling paid to them by the said Joseph Nadin.' The generalities of Arthur's indenture rather confirmed the mystique of the medical profession at this time. 'His masters faithfully he shall serve, their secrets keep, their lawful commands everywhere gladly do; he shall do no damage to his said masters nor see it to be done of others but to his power shall tell or forthwith give warning. He shall not commit fornication nor contract marriage within the said term; he shall not play at cards or dice tables or other unlawful games... he shall neither buy nor sell; he shall not haunt taverns or playhouses nor absent himself from service day or night....'

George Lowe had qualified in 1837, joining Robert Tomlinson in partnership in High Street. Two of Lowe's six sons became doctors, W.G. Lowe becoming prominent in the development of Burton Infirmary with which he was associated for over fifty years until 1921. His surgery was at 5 Horninglow Street (see page 17). His brother, Charles, worked as a general practitioner in Stapenhill, residing at 3 Clay Street.

Stanton Colliery.

_____ 1857

Mr. _____

Bought of Messrs. Nadin

By Mr.

	Tons.	Cwt.	Rate per Ton.	L.	s.	d.
Gross Wt.						
Carriage,						
Neat,....						

A Nadin's Stanton Colliery weigh bill of 1857. A similar weigh bill of 1876 from Bretby Colliery listed 3 tons ll cwt of coal supplied at 19s per ton to Mr Clamp of Hatton for £2 9s 9d (just under £2.50). Darleys, established in 1827, were already prolific printers of all kinds of labels and trade stationery.

Five

Burton Honours Shakespeare

1864 was the tercentenary of Shakespeare's birth. Stratford on Avon staged a festival with a pavilion specially erected for the occasion. As well as some Shakespearean performances events included a banquet, fireworks, a fancy dress ball, two sermons, an ascent of Mr Coxwell's balloon and a recital of Handel's *Messiah*.

Burton on Trent marked the occasion with even greater eccentricity by staging foot races at Ordish's Farm, 'some two thousand spectators cheering Mr W. Lathbury and Mr Pimblett to victories.' The biggest cheer, however, seems to have gone to 'a gentlemen of some 16 stone' who tried to leap across a brook and landed in the middle of it. Perhaps the highlight of these rustic capers came in a short speech by Mr Ordish himself, worthy of being recorded. He said that he gave the use of his farm 'for old Shakespeare's sake.' He liked old Shakespeare. Old Shakespeare was a good old cock. A man after his own heart. And whether his spirit was in Elysium or on Ordish's pasture ground, he hoped this treat would do him good. He hoped he would take it as it was meant. And if he lived another hundred years, he'd 'gi'e 'im another do.' At least it was a genuine old yeoman's tribute to the bard.

In July 1863 a Midlands photographic firm, John Burton & Sons, opened an agency in the town. Their studio was on the premises of H. Steer, jeweller, at 19 High Street (the present, rebuilt location of Lancaster and Thorpe, opticians). Attendance was on Thursdays and Saturdays and any Burtonians having a photograph taken at this time would have found (perhaps on the back of a *carte de visite*, ancestor of the picture postcard), the words: 'Official Photographers to the Stratford Tercentenary Festival.' Another possible local souvenir was advertised by Caleb Goodman of 13 High Street - a site which in more recent times became Cantors, furnishers. As early as 1851 Mr Goodman listed himself as a newsagent - although there was no regular local newspaper until the *Burton on Trent Times and General Advertiser* of 1855. In this paper at Tercentenary time, April 1864, Mr Goodman advertised Part One of *The Young Ladies' Journal* which, as well as special supplements on fashion and fancy work, also contained: 'Eight Pages of Music entitled "The Bard of Avon Quadrilles" in Commemoration of the Shakespeare Tercentenary.' One wonders if any copies survive and whether these graceful dances were ever featured during a ball at the old Town Hall in the Market Place.

The quality of this original old photograph of Ordish's Farm is such that the tip of Christ Church spire (1844) can be identified beyond the roof, left of the chimney. The view dates from shortly before demolition when the area was developed in the 1870s. Built as Bond End Grange in about 1649, it was later known as Bond End Farm, then Ordish's Farm. It stood on Pinfold Lane which led to Common Side; these became Park Street and Dale Street in the 1860s. The farm stood among meadows in the area which became Ordish Street.

Christ Church itself provides one of the town's earliest authenticated photographic views according to the information appended to this scene of the parsonage: 'From a photograph by R. Wilson, July 1857.' The foundation stone of Christ Church was laid, following an elaborate ceremonial procession, by the first Marquess of Anglesey, of Waterloo fame, on 26 September 1843. The Marquess had donated the land for church, school and parsonage, the latter costing £724 15s 11d to build. It was badly damaged when the Parish Room was demolished in the Zeppelin raid of 31 January 1916 during a mission meeting, six people being killed.

Completing the Shakespearean theme, later performances in Burton usually took place in St George's Hall and then at the Opera House, where Sir Frank Benson and his Company were among those offering a week's repertoire of Shakespearean plays during several visits to the town. In 1937 the Burton Shakespeare Society was inaugurated and initially held its meetings at the Shakespeare Inn (29 Victoria Crescent). They staged *The Merchant of Venice* in 1939 and resumed productions in 1947, performing annually throughout the boom years of amateur drama that followed the war.

This Darley's proof copy of an advertisement for 1857 shows that commercial photography was already established in the town. Mr Maginn had 3,000 copies printed for publicity but it should be noted that the emphasis is on portraits with no mention of photographic views, few of which can be dated before the early 1860s when J.S. Simnett began to record the local scene. As a sideline the redoubtable Mr Maginn was also a phrenologist - 'Your fortune read by the bumps on your head' - and a copy survives of the Phrenological Register by Mr J.I. Maginn, Artist.

MR. MAGINN,

The unrivalled Photographer

OF IMPERISHABLE LIKENESSES,

TAKES PORTRAITS FROM ONE SHILLING,

That are perfectly Life-like,

Not daubed and distorted by the would be Photographer, but true representations of cherished individuals, which is evidenced by the success that has attended him in Burton, at his Rooms

NEXT DOOR TO THE

MIDLAND HOTEL,

STATION STREET.

About pretenders in the art he says nothing, but leaves it to the Public to decide. Compare Specimens, and judge for yourselves. Do not be misled by misrepresentation.

N.B.—Remember these Portraits are taken IN DOORS, thereby avoiding the danger of catching cold.

Theatre, Station Street.

GREAT TEST OF TALENT!

Whereas numerous solicitations have been made to witness Messrs. NOAKES & BUTLER perform the same characters; those gentlemen have consented that it shall take place this day TUESDAY and to-morrow WEDNESDAY, January 20th and 21st, in Shakespeare's tragedy of

OTHELLO

TUESDAY,

Othello, Mr. Butler.   Iago, Mr. Noakes.

WEDNESDAY,

Othello, Mr. Noakes.   Iago, Mr. Butler.

Pit 6d.   Gallery 3d.

N.B. See, believe, & judge impartially.

[Darley, Printer.

(.500) January 20th

Returning to Shakespeare, this poster is also of 1857. From the Blue Posts many play performances moved to a hall at the rear of the Staffordshire Knot in Station Street. The mind boggles at the thought of Victorian Burtonians flocking to watch *Othello* two nights running, but at least there were popular prices and the hall could only be reached through the pub! Later this 'theatre' became the home of the popular Wilson's Music Hall, now with a separate entrance to attract a better class of audience. Ingeniously, however, patrons could have twopence returned in drinks if they chose to adjourn to the bar.

Six

A Demon Bowler

Also in 1864, Burton contributed a star bowler to the All England cricket team touring Australia. R.C. Tinley 'our noted townsman' wrought havoc with his 'slows' for the England XI against various teams of XXII players, 'completely flabbergasting the plucky Australians.' On 16 July a presentation was made to him at the Burton Cricket Club ground of a gold watch with 'unique cricket and XXX beer barrel appendages.' The following year, on 20 July, an XI of All England played XXII of Burton over three days. All England scored 79 and 80; the Burton '22' scoring 71 and 30. R.C. Tinley took 21 Burton wickets. He had become Burton's professional player in 1854; later he had a shop in Station Street specialising in cricket and fishing equipment. Burton Cricket Club itself dates back to at least 1827 and during Tinley's period played such clubs as Sheffield, Manchester, Leicester and Liverpool, as well as entertaining the All England XI on three occasions.

W. Ferguson (Scorer). E. L. A'Beckett. P. M. Hornibrook. W. L. Kelly (Manager). T. W. Wall. A. Hurwood. T. Howard (Treasurer). A. F. Kippax. A. Fairfax. V. Y. Richardson (Vice-Captain). W. M. Woodfull (Captain). W. H. Ponsford. D. Bradman. A. Jackson. C. W. Walker. C. V. Grimmett. W. A. Oldfield.
THE AUSTRALIAN TEST TEAM, 1930 are wearing JAEGER Shirts, Sweaters, Trousers, etc. specially supplied for the present tour.
(Photo by Bolland.) (Taken specially for the Jaeger Co. Ltd.)

It was a different story in 1930 when Don Bradman was a member of the powerful Australian side touring England. Their only local appearance was on a publicity postcard issued by Ellis's the tailors. This surviving Burton shop was actually established in 1864, the year of R.C. Tinley's England exploits. Local cricketers were advised that Ellis's stocked the same immaculate Jaegar sweaters as those worn by the tourists.

This High Street scene of 1903 is full of interest. In addition to showing Ellis's old shop on the Market Place corner (their present building was erected in 1908), there is one of the new trams which started running on 3 August 1903, a fine steam lorry, and the horse drawn delivery cart of Radford's bakery, then based in Moor Street. Cycles and pedestrians contribute to make this one of the liveliest town scenes. The stripes of George Ronde's ice cream stall attract attention as would the rich aromas that people still recall coming from Oakden's grocery near to the cart.

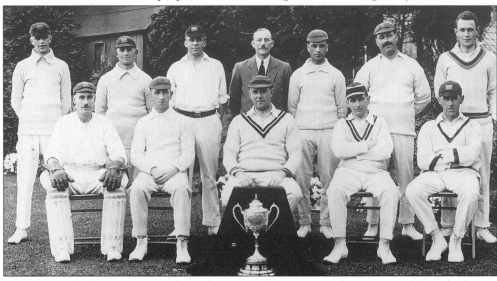

An Ernest Abrahams' photograph of the successful Marston, Thompson and Evershed team which won the Burton Brewery Cricket Cup 1924-25. From left to right, rear: L.C. Bunting, J. Green, H.L. Tomlinson, W. Taylor (hon sec), C. Smith, J. Starbuck, L.A. Taylor. Front: F. Mortimer, W. Marshall (holder of wartime Military Cross), F.G. Peach (captain, Mayor of Burton 1958), J.T.H. Jackson, J.H. Pollard. More of Ellis's cricket wear is no doubt on display here!

Seven

High Society

King Edward VII visited the area on a number of occasions through his friendship with Lord Burton. His visit to the Bass Brewery on 22 February 1902 received wide publicity, but this photograph records the aristocratic guests attending a private house party at Rangemore Hall on 5 January 1907. Posed out of doors, they had no doubt hoped - especially those without coats - that local photographer Ernest Abrahams would speedily complete the customary souvenir group picture. At the back, from left to right: Austro-Hungarian Ambassador, Lady Alice Stanley. Rear row: Hon Col Legge, Marquis of Soveral, Duchess of Devonshire, Mr Bass, Lord Elcho, Miss J. Thornewill, HM The Queen, Lord Burton, Lady Mar and Kellie, Prince Henry of Pless. Front row: Lady Noreen Bass, Miss Muriel Wilson, Lady Desborough, Lady de Grey, the King, Lady Burton, Princess Henry of Pless, Mrs G. Keppel, Miss Thornewill.

The drawing room at Rangemore where the guests would spend much of their time. The other side of this event is well told on the back of a postcard view of the hall posted on 24 January 1907. 'Dear Miss B, thanks for nice present at Xmas. Sorry I've not written before but have been so busy and it's such a job to get even a P.C. The X marks top of kitchen.' This telling comment, written soon after the house party, was almost certainly sent to a fellow servant, Miss Bosworth, c/o 49 Mount Street, Park Lane, close to Lord Burton's London house.

The activities of Lord Burton and his family always attracted much local interest and innumerable views showed Rangemore Hall, its interior and grounds, and scenes of events there, as well as the royal visits. This photograph shows Lord Burton's London residence, Chesterfield House, at the corner of Curzon Street and South Audley Street, Mayfair (built 1750, demolished for flats 1937). His lordship died here on 1 February 1909, his body being brought back by train to Barton and Walton station for interment at Rangemore.

Lord Burton also rented Glenquoich, a hunting lodge in Inverness-shire where his guests again included the King. One of Lord Burton's less successful enterprises was financial backing for the Invergarry and Fort Augustus Railway built through this sparsely populated region. When the Highland Railway withdrew from operating it (1903-7), an agreement was signed at Bass's High Street offices for the North British Company to take over, but the line never prospered. Glenquoich outlasted the railway but was demolished in 1955.

Following Lord Burton's death on 1 February 1909, a memorial statuette was produced for sale locally within the month. The statuette, marked A. Willis, Sculptor, Stoke on Trent, is dated 26 February. The long-established firm of Tresises (1859) were also stationers and proprietors of the halfpenny evening newspaper the *Burton Evening Gazette* (until 1931) and two 1d weekly papers, the *Guardian* and the *Chronicle*. The statuette, costing the equivalent of 12½p, seems to have sold well locally, reflecting the esteem with which his lordship was regarded.

There was a great opportunity for the public to be present at an aristocratic occasion when the Primrose League held one of its big country house events at Drakelowe Hall on 27 July 1907. Sir Robert Gresley as host was in the chair, and speakers included the Marquess of Londonderry and the Duke of Marlborough. The long terrace, only recently added along the front of the hall, served as a platform for the principal guests, with the lawns sweeping down to the Trent as a fine viewpoint for the crowds who supported this event dressed up to enjoy the summer sunshine.

One country house about which the general public knew very little was Calke Abbey, now a popular National Trust property. The Harpur Crewe family tended towards privacy and seclusion so that there was wide local interest when Sir Vauncey's daughter, Hilda, was married at Ticknall Church on 4 February 1918 to Colonel Godfrey Mosley of Willington, partner in a Derby firm of solicitors. Here, villagers and estate workers gather in the churchyard for the couple's departure after the ceremony. Mrs Mosley inherited the property in 1924.

Eight
Townsfolk

A foundation stone, dated 28 June 1899, can still be seen today, low down by the first house on the left, in Balfour Street. It was laid by R.F. Ratcliff Esq, shortly before he became the local MP, to start an ambitious project by the Artisans' Dwelling Company to build seventy-two houses here and sixty-three in Craven Street over the period 1900-1902. A five-roomed house cost £150. The contractor was Harry Edwards of Blackpool Street. The architect was Thomas Jenkins (Mayor 1909-10) who also designed the former Electric Theatre in High Street. The corner shop, first run by Fred Grout, is still open. The superimposed domestic scene fits in well with a slogan used by the Burton Corporation Gas Works: 'Meals cooked by gas are hard to surpass.'

These are employees of Henry Edwards Ltd, some of whom would have helped to build Balfour Street. It is likely that a works outing around 1909 combined pleasure with a certain amount of business interest because they obviously visited an industrial site, possibly Staton's alabaster mines at Fauld.

Coopers were once among the highest paid local employees, practising their trade at all the principal breweries or in some half dozen independent cooperages around the town. They organised their own society with both trade union and friendly society functions. This group of Allsopps coopers is certainly representative of all ages and experience. It includes apprentices (one for every five or six men) serving a 5 year term, culminating with the initiation ceremony known as 'trussing in'. At one time Allsopps employed 120 coopers out of the 1,000 or so working locally around 1900. This scene shows their new brewery cooperage which extended from Station Street to Brook Street. A lot of the coopers' work was in repairing rather than making casks as these were often machine-made, as at Bass's famous steam cooperage, but with over 500,000 Bass barrels to be maintained there was still plenty of work. It all changed with the introduction of metal casks; no more apprentices were taken on and as the old coopers retired the cooperages closed, so that today this is a lost Burton craft.

It was good while it lasted! In 1921 Crosse and Blackwell acquired the Branston National Machine Gun factory which, in spite of its name, failed to produce any machine guns before the First World War ended. Crosse and Blackwell stayed long enough to establish the name of Branston Pickle but the firm returned to London in 1924/5. They had employed some 600 people, the majority of them women. This scene shows the Town Hall during the firm's first annual ball in 1922.

Just some of the people of Burton who packed into the Market Place for the Proclamation of King George V on 9 May 1910. All such formal ceremonies were attended by enthusiastic crowds even when there were no processions or associated events. Mr West has been favoured with a free advertisement for his oyster saloon but with oysters out of season from May until September, one wonders what else was on offer.

In March 1912 Mr and Mrs Elliott, well known evangelists, held mission services at Parker Street Methodist Chapel attracting big attendances. A young couple, the Elliotts' publicity photograph shows them rather soulfully seated side by side under the quotation: 'Let us exalt his name together.' This scene in the chapel suggests that it was standing room only.

The crowd here is attending the stone laying ceremony for the new schoolroom for George Street Chapel on 28 March 1893. Among bricks laid on this occasion were many bearing the initials of Sunday School scholars. The earlier schoolroom behind the chapel was demolished and the new building replaced an old malting.

The YMCA was very popular locally, providing sporting, social and spiritual activities based, from 1901, in the High Street building which stretched right back to Friars Walk and included the former Anglesey Hall, which survives. All the front buildings were demolished in 1972 but the open space seen today down Anglesey Passage was the site of the well equipped gymnasium, where this photograph of the junior department was taken in 1913.

Burton was occasionally featured on cigarette cards, a view of the boat houses from Trent Bridge being one example. In a series featuring football teams, card no. 80 issued by the Ardath Tobacco Company showed Winshill Amateurs FC, listing their performances in 1935/6 when they won the Burton and District League Senior Championship and were semi-finalists in the Challenge Cup. Back row, from left to right: S. Wilson (trainer), J. Goy (committee), F. Brittain (secretary), H. Sparrow, C. Lovatt, F. Twamley, C. Thornewell, T. Wright, C. Warren, R. Moore (chairman), L. Bladon, T. Goy (assistant trainer), E.J. Wilson (committee). Front row: G. Stevens, H. Cotton, R. Jones (captain), J. Dunn, A. Gooch, F. Miller.

Voluntarily present at many public events to render assistance if needed, a local branch of the St John Ambulance Association was formed in 1884. The Burton Division of the St John Ambulance Brigade dates from 1916. Later, Ambulance and Nursing Divisions and a Cadet Force were formed. This photograph records the Burton branch's earlier days.

Revd H.B. Freeman MA was vicar of Burton from 1899 until 1924 and became a very well known local figure. Just before his departure he produced a small volume called *Memories and Reflections* in which he recorded his normal daily exercise: 'Since 1 January 1918, I have walked from my house (the vicarage was in Ordish Street) round the Burton and Ferry Bridges, a distance of a few yards under two and a quarter miles, exactly 2,208 times.'

This looks like the work of a street photographer, usually associated with the seaside. The casual snapshot of the ladies shopping in Station Street suggests the late 1920s. There is still horse traffic, the freedom to park anywhere and, of course, plain brown paper and string for parcels in these days before plastic bags. Bailey's clock shows twenty to twelve so it is nearly time for lunch at Boots' Cafe!

A wonderful Christmas or birthday for this delightful if solemn little girl. Her baby doll can smile at riding in such a handsome replica pram, probably of the early 1920s. This Simnett studio portrait makes a change from one of his many local views.

Nine
Burton's Lost Breweries

In 1888 J.N. Tresise of Station Street, publisher of two local newspapers, produced an album of *Views of Burton on Trent* 'With some of the Principal Breweries and Public Buildings.' It was a publication of high quality and many of its prints have been used at different times because of their interest and value as pictorial records. It was about this time that the expansion of brewing in Burton reached its zenith and there were over thirty breweries of varying sizes in the town, giving employment to over 8,000 men. The Tresise pictures are therefore of special interest and his brewery views show many buildings and scenes that have either completely disappeared or have been greatly changed. We felt that they deserved to be reproduced as a record of the Burton brewery scene at the height of its development.

Bass and Co.'s 'New' Brewery and Maltings as shown in Tresise's book of 1888.

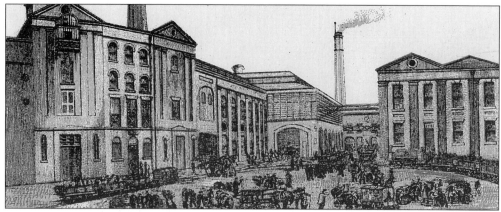

Allsopps Old Brewery, (1842-43), High Street, on the Benjamin Wilson Brewery site (1807). Part of the premises later became Eatoughs, shoe manufacturers. All buildings have now gone.

Bass Old Brewery, High Street (1777), rebuilt 1876-78, demolished 1971; offices, as shown, by 1882.

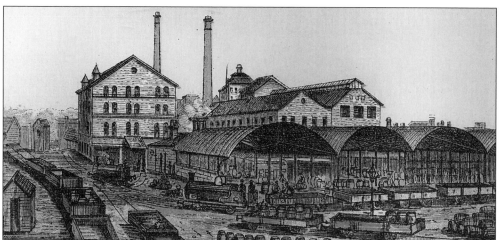

Worthingtons, High Street (1760) - a rebuilding of 1860; demolished 1960s. Bass merged with Worthington in 1926.

Charringtons, Abbey Street, 1872; closed 1926; demolished *c.* 1970 for a new B & Q site, but the Leopard Inn (left) remains.

Ind Coope, Station Street, 1856, merged with Allsopp's in 1934.

Robinsons, Union Street, 1863; went to Ind Coope in 1918, later demolished.

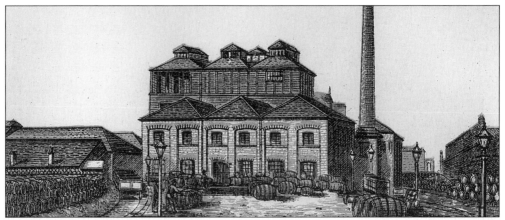

'Crescent' Brewery (Victoria Crescent), Cooper's, 1865, was taken over by Salts then became industrial premises, now gone.

Mann, Crossman and Paulin (London), Shobnall Road, 1874; vacated *c.* 1896. Albion, a non-brewing company, leased the premises and sold on, hence the name Albion Brewery; it became Marston's from 1898.

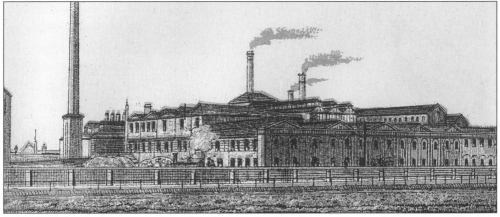

Salts (1800), High Street; these buildings, *c.* 1870, became part of Bass in 1927; now demolished.

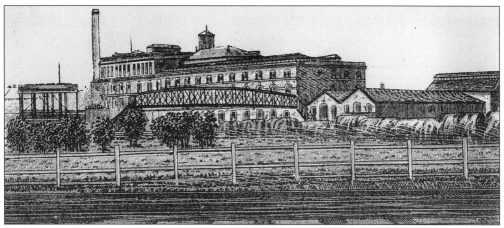

Truman, Hanbury and Buxton, Derby Street (1873), formerly Phillip's Brewery (1860), closed in 1970 and demolished.

Thompson's Brewery, Horninglow Street, 1840, near Bargates, but this scene shows premises near the main railway (1867), later Hodges, builders. Thompson joined with Marston in 1898.

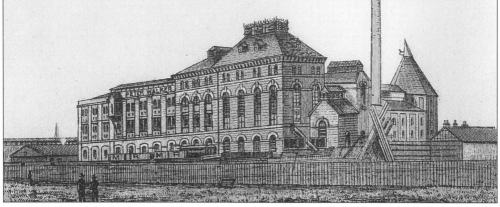

Peter Walker, Warrington and Burton, Clarence Street, 1880, closed 1926-27 but 'Goat' maltings preserved.

Allsopps converted their 'old' brewery for lager production, with new plant from America, in 1899. This scene shows their lager cellar. Allsopps advertised widely, especially by using personal recommendation and we like the 'unsolicited' letter of 1903 to the *Liverpool Courier* from Madame Albani, an opera singer. 'I have been drinking it nearly every day at luncheon and dinner... It is always brisk, refreshing and in beautiful condition and I believe it to be very good for the digestion and for the voice.'

Hill & Son's Brewery, Lichfield Street, 1830-90. The name survives over an archway in The Dingle, Stapenhill.

Bell & Co. Brewery, Lichfield Street, 1855, went to Salts in 1902, when owned by Pickering and Roe.

Marston & Son, Dover Road, 1835, Horninglow and Horninglow Street. (See Trouble For Horninglow, page 75 and picture on page 77); Marston Thompson (Albion Brewery) 1898 and Evershed from 1905.

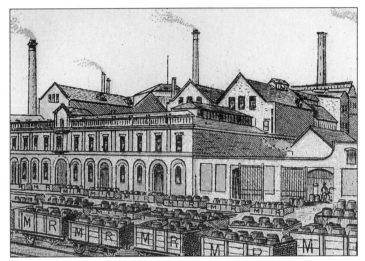

The Burton Brewery Co., High Street, 1842, has an involved history. Originally Wilder's, it went to Worthingtons in 1914 but continued supplying its own licensed properties from Salts. Closed when Bass acquired Salts in 1927, its leases were sold to Ind Coope.

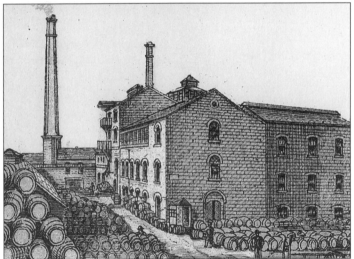

Dawson & Co., Moor Street, 1872-1890. The premises went to Briggs, engineers in 1900, including the Robin Hood beerhouse which became offices.

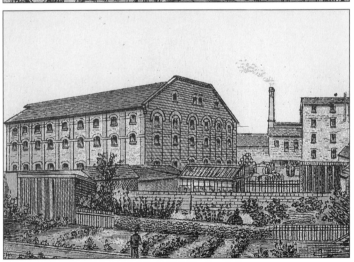

Green & Clarkson, Victoria Street, operated under various names from 1872-88. Used by Walkers as 'The Midland Brewery' in 1890 it was put to other uses by early 1900 and has now gone.

Brindley's Brewery. John Allen Brindley, former Worthington head brewer, started his own brewery in New Street around 1874; it became part of Ind Coope in 1920 and the premises were demolished in about 1969.

Eadie's Brewery, Cross Street, 1855, ceased production in 1933 when absorbed by Bass but remained as the Bass-Worthington wines and spirits centre until 1963.

Sykes of Liverpool built Kimmersitch Street Brewery in 1880, which became Everards from 1898-1984. After an unsuccessful project as a Heritage Brewery and Museum it is now derelict.

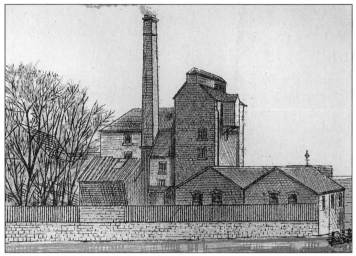

Boddington & Co. (Manchester), Meadow Lane, 1870-85. This was a brief operation because their well had no Burton brewing properties, as it only supplyed filtered valley water.

Evershed's 'Angel' Brewery, Bank Square, 1854, was joined with Marston, Thompson in 1905. The buildings were demolished in the 1960s.

A.B. Walker's Brewery. Sir Andrew Barclay Walker was the proprietor of breweries in Warrington, Burton and elsewhere. When Burton production ceased, Bass acquired Shobnall Brewery in 1923 and it became English Grains, blocking any prospective new brewery development.

Looking at these old brewery buildings we realised that among the thousands of local scenes we have amassed, there is not a single one of an old Burton brewery or maltings actually under construction. Many, of course, have been photographed in more recent times either derelict or in the course of being demolished. We now include, therefore, the nearest example we can find - the rebuilding of the severely fire-damaged Wood Street maltings of Peach and Company by the firm of Henry Edwards Ltd of Blackpool Street. The fire broke out just before midnight on 7 July 1908 and was one of the most spectacular of all local fire disasters, providing, by all accounts, great spectator sport. The maltings were full at the time and smouldering grain required the presence of firemen on the scene for several weeks afterwards before the complete reconstruction of the gutted building could take place.

The premises of J.N. Tresise, Nos 186-187 Station Street, publisher of the brewery views of 1888. This business still thrives in the town today, having greatly expanded into all aspects of the printing trade. The offices for the firm's three newspapers were situated here and they also produced invaluable directories as well as being stationers, printers and bookbinders. Their bookbinding works at the time of the photograph, around 1912, was in Union Street. The shop also displays their range of picture postcards on either side of the doorway.

Ten

A Musical Interlude

The mid-nineteenth century saw many organisations, societies and other groups first established in the town. Among them was the Burton Musical Society, founded by Mr L.F. Day, who also acted as a local impresario, arranging classical concerts. In January 1857 Mr Day begged 'to announce to his friends and the inhabitants of Burton and its neighbourhood that he proposes giving a concert in the Town Hall for which he has engaged the services of the *Anemonic Union*'. His patrons were offered orchestral and vocal items by Mozart, Verdi, Beethoven, Meyerbeer, Donizetti, Rossini and others for which reserved seats cost 3s 6d (17½p). A postscript advised that 'there will be an Attendant in the Cloak Room for the convenience of Ladies wishing to remove their Bonnets.' This was very much the upper end of the local entertainment provided, contrasting with the melodramas mentioned earlier down at the Blue Posts. It is interesting that Mr Day's lowest charge of 1s (5p) was for the Promenade. Judging by the many press complaints in the 1860s about the uncomfortable, hard seats in Burton's old Town Hall, there could well have been patrons who stood up for a rest! L.F. Day was a teacher of music at 40 Lichfield Street and, as Simnett's photograph shows, lived to a ripe old age, this picture dating nearly fifty years after he staged his grand concert. Number 40 Lichfield Street subsequently passed to Percy Salmon and it was at the rear of the premises that he produced, for a few years, the Salmon motor car.

Mr L.F. Day.

Burton's two attractive Victorian bandstands no longer exist and these scenes belong to their heyday when there were many local musicians to play at popular concerts. Ten or more bands were often listed in the order of procession for carnivals and galas. The A38 by-pass cut through the Outwoods Recreation Ground site which had been developed in 1884. Stapenhill Pleasure Grounds were laid out in 1865 and this bandstand site is still clearly recognisable, but increasing traffic noise made it difficult to enjoy the stirring strains of *The Entry of the Gladiators* and it was dismantled in 1962.

BAND STAND,
BURTON-ON-TRENT.

Alongside the demolished George Hotel in High Street was the shop of another well known musical personality, A.V. Cresser. Apart from supplying every kind of musical item from sheet music to organs, Mr Cresser, possessing a rich bass voice, was much in demand as a performer. One of his fine new pianos for the front parlour (usually priced in guineas) would cost from £12 to £15. Early gramophones were available from £2. Mr Cresser also promoted high class concerts, with the big advantage of the new Town Hall being available for performances. Among them was the visit of the Beecham Orchestra on 15 October 1909, conducted by the up-and-coming Thomas Beecham.

Prominent as a conductor in Edwardian Burton was Mr John Frost, a schoolmaster who lived in Blackpool Street. He was, for many years, musical director for productions of Burton Operatic Society and was also a conductor of local choirs.

Another schoolmaster greatly in demand as a singer was H.J. Cumper, always affectionately known as 'Keggy'. He appeared in innumerable concerts and Operatic Society shows and is seen here attired for his role in their 1924 production of *The Geisha*.

We can now invite readers to try out for themselves a piece of music with local associations - part of Frederick Cotton's spirited hunting song *The Meynell Hunt*.

Drakelowe Hall, home of the Gresleys, was demolished in 1934. Previously, in 1931, there had been a great sale of the contents. This photograph shows the music room in the 1890s but it was little altered when the auctioneers moved in. Someone acquired the maroon Wilton carpet, 16 x 13 ft, for £9.45 and an Axminster carpet underneath for £3.30. The revolving bookcase made £5.50 and the 10 ft silk damask curtains with fittings fetched £2.60. The early sixteenth century Italian commode sold for £15.75, while the room's high spot, the French Renaissance *dressoir*, which commanded a full page plate in the catalogue, made £68.25. On the left is the Bechstein boudoir grand piano in rosewood case and this, bought for £48, is still being played and enjoyed today.

The Salvation Army was established in Burton in 1886 and the first local band was formed in 1890. As well as open air meetings around the area the band was often part of processions and gala occasions. Young People's Bands, the Singing Company and the Songster Brigade all played a part in maintaining a notable local musical tradition which continues today. Many local Corps records were unfortunately lost when the Brook Street Citadel was badly damaged by fire on 5 October 1942.

In the years just before the Second World War the Farrington sisters, Olive, Joan and Betty were popular local entertainers playing, between them, the banjo, cello, piano, xylophone and trombone, Betty playing the latter instrument with Len Reynolds' Dance Band. The girls made several broadcasts from Birmingham for the BBC's *Children's Hour* on radio and also travelled extensively with the Salvation Army bands. This photograph of Olive and Joan dates from 1936/7.

Eleven
Going Shopping

Burton's shopping streets in Edwardian days largely consisted of small, privately owned stores, while many people used the corner shops which were a feature of the grid development of the town's housing areas. Most food products were sold loose and were weighed and wrapped as required, which helped those on low incomes who could buy small quantities. People were, indeed, often suspicious of pre-packed food. There were no regulated shopping hours so you purchased as and when required - or when money was available, although credit was sometimes allowed until pay day and pawn shops might be frequented in times of need.

Those who were better off could send for provisions or call in person when an assistant offered them a chair in the shop, errand boys later delivering the order. Windows tended to be crammed with a jumbled mixture of wares while poultrymen and butchers displayed stock well exposed to the elements. Refrigeration was virtually unknown unless by ice blocks, and there were few hygiene requirements, with little attention given to the handling of food or the washing of hands.

Family budgets varied widely, some families perhaps subsisting on as little as 10s or 15s a week (50p to 75p). Around 27s a week (£1.35) would be that of quite a well-to-do working family but out of that there might be, say, 30p for rent and 15p for two bags of coal. A weekly menu would mainly feature bread, porridge, bacon, mutton, cheese, potatoes and tea, often boosted by vegetables, most local houses having a compact but useful garden. Jam, butter, suet, rice, cocoa, fish and fruit were additions to give a change of diet. Feeding babies and children, along with such extras as boots and clothes, soap, sewing cotton, black lead for the cooking range and items like salt, yeast or baking powder, all called for careful management by the housewife with not much left over to cover illness or to buy luxuries.

The Market Hall from J.N. Tresise's book of 1888.

The name Robirch is now widely known. It had its beginnings after two local pork butchers, A.J. Roberts and J.H. Birch, both subsequently councillors and mayors of the town, went into partnership. In the early 1900s this was Roberts' shop at 184/5 High Street, the last building in a block of shops where the Abbey Arcade now stands. To the right were the remains of Burton Abbey gateway and everything was cleared in 1927. Already at the time of this photograph, A.J. Roberts had branches in Station Street and on Branston Road.

This attractive building with a clock tower, 76 Mosley Street, as it was in the mid-Edwardian period as Squire's Grocery Stores. They only had a short occupancy before the premises were acquired by Roberts and Birch. To the rear they established their sausage and pork pie factory, adding to the varied aromas that greeted travellers on Burton railway station. From here the firm continued expanding to become Robirch.

Carey M. Livens was also a councillor and mayor of the town and his shop was at 172 High Street, next to the George Hotel, the archway of which just appears on the right. This block of buildings was rebuilt in the late 1920s. Livens stocked a wide range of ironmongery and manufactured railway milk churns and dairy items. He advertised the services of electrician, gas fitter, bell-hanger, locksmith, hot water engineer and metal sheet worker. For cash payments there was a fixed discount of one penny in the shilling.

Hallam the chemist had claims to be Burton's oldest established shop (1768). The photograph shows their premises at 22 High Street before they moved in the 1930s to No. 44, near Worthington's crossing, previously used as the Labour Exchange. As well as being chemists they dealt in photographic items, oils and paints, and were suppliers of all kinds of seeds. They were also sole makers of Hallam's Burton Grass Destroyer!

Typically, at the crossing of Princess Street and Albert Street there were three corner shops and a public house, the Admiral Benbow. In 1911 one shop was that of Alexander G. Pye who was listed as a chemist and dentist. Until 1921 a dental practitioner had to be registered, but would not have had the course of training required to be classed as a dental surgeon.

On another nearby corner (Princess Street and Edward Street) was the branch shop of William Fox of Uxbridge Street, outfitter, jeweller and - of some importance in this working class area - pawnbroker. The three brass balls sign appears over each frontage. The mass array of clothing was at prices appropriate to the locality: 'The Popular Working Men's Outfitters For Bargains.' Made to measure suits were from the equivalent of £1.25 with trousers from 15p and shirts from 5p.

Many streets had their own dairyman (or cow keeper) and milk seller of which J.W. Campion of 217 Stafford Street is one example. Four pints of milk could be bought for $2\frac{1}{2}$p. The shop window contains an additional but unidentifiable assortment of items. Forty dairy establishments were listed around the town in 1911.

With horses still predominant in Edwardian Burton, saddle and harness makers were of great importance and nine of them were kept busy before the First World War, but with increasing motor traffic the number was already down to four by the mid-1920s. A.E. Waddon of 185 Horninglow Street manufactured harness, leggings and bags on the premises, supplied belting for machinery, and called for and delivered, free of charge, orders and repairs of leather goods.

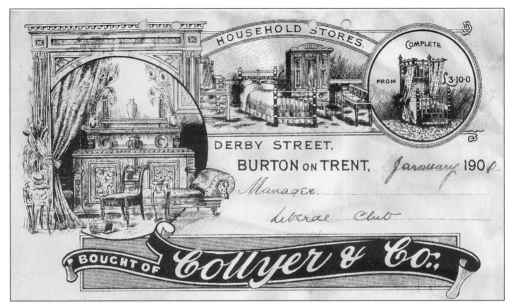

An impressive display of the latest designs in furnishings at the start of the twentieth century. Collyer & Co. were located at Aristo House, Derby Street, opposite to Byrkley Street. Later it became W.H. Ball, followed by E. Tye. The site is now part of Kwik Save. Features of this general household store included hair mattresses to order; special designs for brass, iron and French bedsteads, bars fitted and smoke rooms upholstered.

A classic example of how to use up every available inch of window space. Apart from filling his window, the Edwardian hatter was kept busy. It is quite rare when looking at photographs of the period to pick out anyone not wearing headgear. W. Oldham's shop was at 158 Station Street and he was described as a 'Gentlemen's Silk and Felt Hatter, Hosier and Glover'.

Although most local shops were still private businesses in Edwardian times, branches of national shops were being established, in particular provision shops, under a branch manager. One of the earliest was Pearks who took over the premises of Midland Grocery at 8 High Street, remaining there for many years, This was the corner of little Fennel Street which led round Bank Square to Dame Paulet's almshouses, all demolished for the Cooper Shopping Centre. Fennel Street was an old name reflecting the days of Burton Abbey nearby, when the monks cultivated herbs for culinary use.

If you were disillusioned with Burton this could be the shop window to study - A.J. Nixon's Shipping Agency at 69 Union Street (later at 1 Uxbridge Street). Here was news of assisted passage for emigrants to the Dominions and Colonies and various cruises to choose from, such as Norway from £1 a day. In the *Travel Handbook and Calendar* for 1910 other offers included a three-week tour through Italy for £22 or twelve days in Germany for £16 including your ticket for the Oberammergau *Passion Play*.

71

Fringe districts of the town all had their own shops, usually able between them to supply most local needs and often providing a delivery service or daily round of essentials like fresh milk and bread. This is 99 Nelson Street, Winshill, when occupied by C. Harper, grocer, baker and off licence, with his own horse and cart for door to door trade. A surviving bill for home bread deliveries over two months in 1899 by a Stapenhill baker, lists forty-four loaves costing the equivalent of 1p per loaf.

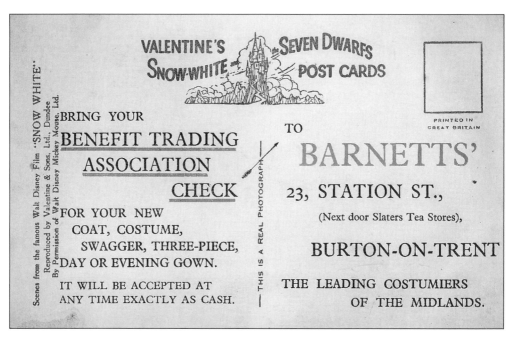

VALENTINE'S SNOW-WHITE — the SEVEN DWARFS POST CARDS

PRINTED IN GREAT BRITAIN

Scenes from the famous Walt Disney Film "SNOW WHITE". Reproduced by Valentine & Sons, Ltd., Dundee. By Permission of Walt Disney Mickey Mouse, Ltd.

THIS IS A REAL PHOTOGRAPH

BRING YOUR
BENEFIT TRADING
ASSOCIATION
CHECK
FOR YOUR NEW
COAT, COSTUME,
SWAGGER, THREE-PIECE,
DAY OR EVENING GOWN.

IT WILL BE ACCEPTED AT
ANY TIME EXACTLY AS CASH.

TO
BARNETTS'
23, STATION ST.,
(Next door Slaters Tea Stores),

BURTON-ON-TRENT

THE LEADING COSTUMIERS
OF THE MIDLANDS.

Does anyone still have a Twopenny Tinker Repair Kit tucked away at the back of a shed? In June 1918 A.S. Wright & Sons established their Stapenhill works in an iron shed in Astil Street (actually at the rear of the corner shop at 30 Woods Lane). They produced liquid glues for woodwork and aircraft parts (perhaps encouraged by the Navarro Aircraft Company having set up in Park Street during the war); a clear glue called Stix-It; and, most successful of all, Twopenny Tinker, for repairing all kinds of enamelled ware, iron and tin goods in an age of 'make do and mend'. Sales of this ran into millions and production continued between the wars. The site was later occupied by lock-up garages. Nearby was a creamery making hand-made butter. With no such refinements as air conditioning, work began here at 4.00 am to finish while the day was still cool and Alf Moss recalls local children helping to wrap up the butter before school time.

Opposite: In the 1930s there were three Trading Associations listed in Burton, the Benefit T.A. being based at 5/6 Waterloo Street. This Station Street costumiers is inviting custom using Valentine's *Snow White* postcards which showed photographic scenes from the highly successful full length animated cartoon film produced by Walt Disney in 1937 and, with its catchy tunes, all the rage! These cards are now much sought after.

The Gift that Pleases

IN most cases the amount of pleasure with which a gift is received does not by any means depend upon its costliness—more often than not the gift that pleases is that which illustrates the degree of sympathy existing between the giver and the recipient.

But, as time passes, the selection of a suitable gift becomes increasingly difficult, and thus it is one so often hears, "**I wish I knew what to give So-and-So.**" Fortunately, though, there is one gift that is always appreciated—a gift that, in fact, the passing of time itself renders ever new, and that is—**A Photograph.**

In its simplest form the Photograph makes an admirable substitute for the ordinary Christmas Card, while, if something more expensive be desired, either a larger size or a miniature could be given.

For the approaching Christmas Season, then, I therefore venture to suggest that you, too, could please your friends by sending them your Photograph. May I make an appointment for a Sitting?

You are probably familiar with the quality of my work, but, if you have not yet seen it, I shall be happy to show you Specimens in all the Latest Styles, if you will favour me with a call at my Studio.

N.B.—There is still an impression that a bright day is essential for Photography; owing, however, to the use of the finest modern Apparatus, good results are guaranteed even on dull winter days.

Ernest Abrahams,
Photographic Artist,
— 116 Station St. —
(foot of Bridge).
BURTON - ON - TRENT.

Four delightful studies of local youngsters add interest to this Ernest Abrahams advertisement for Christmas 1908, when he felt the need to stress that with 'modern apparatus' a bright day was no longer essential for studio photography. He was still located at 116 Station Street, at the foot of Station Bridge in 1929, when his advertising also listed Doris F. Lean as Studio Operator and Colourist and Robert Kellett as Outdoor and Commercial Operator. He offered a range of 'Cameras and Sundries for Amateurs - Let a 'Professional' have your developing and printing.'

Twelve
Trouble for Horninglow

In the summer of 1907 there was great local interest in the affair of the Horninglow Smell. Eventually, in the High Court, the Vicar of St John's, Revd S.O. Miller of 5 Rolleston Road, sought damages and an injunction in the matter of 'nauseating smells' arising from the cattle food works of F. Gothard (trading as Wardle & Co.) on Rolleston Road corner.

Residents and local medical and scientific experts were called to London to give evidence for or against, after which the judge announced that he felt there had been some nuisance and granted an injunction with costs (suspended for two months) restraining the defendants from carrying on their works in such a way as to cause a nuisance. Mr Gothard promptly ordered the works to close and employees to be given a week's notice. It was when this outcome became known that events came to a head in Horninglow.

From 7.00 pm on Wednesday 8 May a noisy demonstration began. At first children and youths paraded beating cans, blowing tin whistles and shouting 'opprobrious epithets' directed at the vicar and those witnesses who had supported him. By 9.00 pm many more people had assembled and as trams and cabs from the station began to discharge witnesses there were alternate cheers and boos, with Councillor Coxon and his family subjected to having rubbish flung at their cab and into the garden of their house near the vicarage. Here the crowd was thwarted by the non-arrival of Revd Miller but there were noisy expressions of disapproval and two windows were broken by stones before the police finally cleared the area around 11.00 pm, the mob noisily dispersing after Mr Wood, the works' foreman, was carried home shoulder high to great cheering. The local press headlines proclaimed: 'Disgraceful Scenes at Horninglow; Uproarious Behaviour.'

On Thursday evening crowds again assembled on Rolleson Road corner, about 300 people plainly indicating their intention of demonstrating against the vicar on his return home. 'A substantial police presence' endeavoured to 'control any outburst tending to a riot.' When the vicar's cab approached at 8.45 pm, the crowd rushed to the vicarage, the police containing them but unable to curb the shouting of 'Mob him, mob him', alternating with an ironic chorus of 'Give us this day our daily bread.' The crowd finally drifted away after about an hour.

In a press statement next day Revd S.O. Miller stressed that the last thing he wanted was to put people out of work, but he had paid £610 for his house ten years ago and felt that the smell greatly depreciated its value as well as injuring his health. He had been reluctant to act and hoped that with the injunction suspended, the proprietor could now get things into proper order allowing employees to resume work without detriment to other people.

Friday evening then appeared to be passing quietly with police moving on any 'rough elements' loitering in the vicinity. But at 10.00 pm the whole area was suddenly lit up by the glare from a blazing clerical effigy some 12 or 14 ft high introduced into a field opposite the vicarage and set alight. A large crowd quickly congregated to watch the blaze and cheer before moving off in a fairly orderly manner. As the affair took place on private property the police could only watch proceedings.

Saturday saw a larger police force in action, patrolling the neighbourhood and keeping people moving. Their vigilance was rewarded when they captured a second effigy and material for lighting it close to Councillor Coxon's house. The area was cleared and later that night two men were arrested, one of whom had earlier been recognised when attempting to assemble the second effigy.

Sunday and Monday now passed quietly and on Tuesday there was a well attended meeting at the Plough Inn of residents from the vicinity of the Wardle works. The tone was conciliatory and it was learned that Mr Gothard would carry on the works for the period allowed by the court. It was promised that every effort would be promptly made to effect improvements which would obviate any further cause for complaints and ensure local employment. The works subsequently passed to Sustene Limited of Castle Gresley, cattle food manufacturers.

The Horninglow tram terminus was near St John's Church and here the protesters of 1907 awaited the return of witnesses from the court hearings. The name Wardle & Co. can be seen above the former brewery building on Rolleston Road corner that was at the centre of the case. This scene is around 1904 and also provides a fine picture of tram No. 16, running to Branston Road. Its driver has been identified as Thomas Fleming who lived on Bearwood Hill Road.

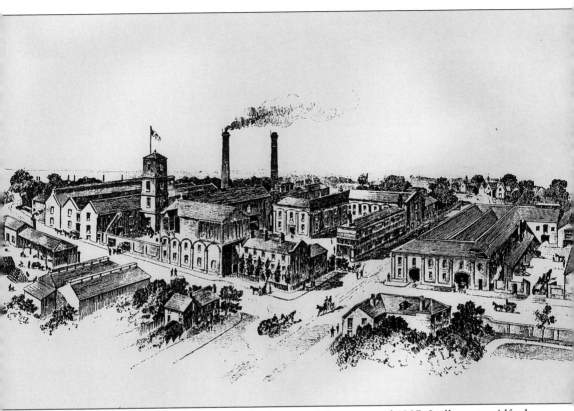

A panoramic view looking down on the focal point of the events of 1907. It illustrates Alfred Barnard's account of his visit to Marston's Horninglow brewery in the 1860s, contained in book two of his *Noted Breweries* volumes. Its location was the highest position of any Burton brewery and was chosen not only for its suitable wells but for its 'pure atmosphere' - an ironic comment considering the events described. The view is from the new St John's Church steeple, possibly from the scaffolding during building. Horninglow Road runs from Burton up the centre of the picture; Rolleston Road is to the right; and to the left is the present Dover Road which was then Patch Lane leading out into open fields. The brewery, built in 1834, occupied both sides of the road. In 1907 the buildings on Rolleston Road had become those of Wardle & Co. and the subject of the court case. Buildings on the opposite side were now those of Richards & Co., maltsters, Marstons having moved out in 1898. Their aroma was of a 'coffee roasting nature' and they were exonerated from causing any offensive smell. The crossroads was the centre of the 1907 disturbances.

Another Horninglow dispute of a different nature over forty years earlier has a much more humorous side to it. On 25/26 August 1862, there was a cricket match between XI of Burton and XXII of Horninglow. It was played on the Broadholme. Horninglow had won the toss and decided to bat when a question arose as to whether a Mr Gregory of Repton should be allowed to play, which 'postponed the start until nearly one o'clock.' The matter was left to Major H. Bass who decided that Mr Gregory should not play. Horninglow XXII then scored 93 and 80, the Burton XI (actually only ten men played) made 79 and 95 for 4 to win by six wickets. 'This was partly owing to the bad fielding of some of the XXII, chance after chance being missed.'

Sadly, press advice a few weeks earlier had not been heeded after Horninglow had entertained Dudley at Horninglow and been beaten by an innings. 'We cannot too strongly impress on the members of the Horninglow Club the desirability of good fielding; many good chances were given which if taken, would have materially altered the state of the game.' The Mr Gregory of the later dispute was, ironically, Horninglow's 'most successful performer with both bat and ball'.

The scene of the 'cricket dispute' though on a much later view, shows the Broadholme wicket well defined along with sightscreen and a modest pavilion. This panorama from the Bass water tower shows the baths and pumping station which have now gone, the length of the Trent Bridge (with tram), the boathouses and a sweeping view up to Winshill Church. The curved bulge to the Hay sidings was originally created to allow shunting of wagons through a right angle to turn them into and out of brewery yards. These cross-lines had been removed before this photograph was taken around 1912.

Thirteen

Up in the Air

A local event that still commands interest is the Aviation Meeting of 1910. In spite of previous coverage we still get enquiries (often from out of town) seeking information, unusual anecdotes or, hopefully, any less familiar photographs. This then is a summary of Burton's modest contribution to the aviation scene between 1910 and the Second World War.

The year 1909 had been significant in flying history. On 25 July Louis Bleriot made his dramatic crossing of the English Channel; Hubert Latham was displaying aeronautical skills at Blackpool; and Doncaster staged the pioneer aviation meeting. It was the French aviators from Doncaster's 1910 event who moved to Burton for Monday 26 September. The impetus came from a local committee chaired by S.H. Evershed, who had earlier built and flown his own aeroplane. They were responsible for hangars, marquees and general arrangements with a London syndicate promoting the event. Bass's Meadow was made available with a marked area cut and levelled. The planes came by rail packed in crates and everything now depended on the wind. If in excess of 15 mph, flying would not be practical so Burtonians took a new interest in Tower Road water tower. A red flag meant that flying would soon begin; a white flag that there might be flying later; no flag that flying was unlikely in the foreseeable future and Burton went back to work.

The planes were reassembled and stored in their canvas hangars and the flyers waited around. With Farman biplanes were Mlle Helene Dutrieu, an attractive young woman who took up flying after being a trick cyclist, Brunneau de Laborie, a monocled aristocrat, and L. Beau. In Bleriot monoplanes were Paul de Lesseps, grandson of the builder of the Suez Canal and Julien Mamet. Emile Ladougne had a Goupy biplane and Marcel Hanriot in his own monoplane was listed but took no part. Monday was a blank day because of strong winds so Burton's first flight was on Tuesday morning when Ladougne made a 2 minute trip. Later, Mamet flew for 13 minutes and reached 1,200 feet. Wednesday saw de Lesseps sweeping over Waterloo Clump, Ladougne making flights with passengers and Mlle Dutrieu flying with Beau as passenger. Beau then flew a Mr Glass as Burton's first public passenger, followed by Mr Barratt and later, the Mayor.

By now excursion trains were running to Burton from all over the Midlands. On Thursday

Mamet circled Lichfield Cathedral and returned at an average speed of 60 mph while de Lesseps reached 4,500 feet then 'lost' himself as it grew dark and landed at Grange Farm near Harlaston, so that a bonfire lit at Burton as a landing beacon was not needed. On Friday de Lesseps took off again, 'missed' Burton and landed in Colwick Park, Nottingham. There were suggestions that these flights were really staged for publicity. Certainly Saturday saw 29,000 people on the meadows for a full programme of flying with many more people watching from vantage points all around the town. Laborie had meanwhile made his impact - quite literally - with Burton's first air crash. On a short test flight on the Friday his plane suddenly shot down to the ground, breaking up, but fortunately leaving Laborie with nothing but a torn trouser leg.

After the programme ended there was a presentation of trophies: Ladougne for longest flight; de Lesseps for highest altitude; Mamet for his Lichfield flight; and Beau for passenger carrying. Helene Dutrieu received a cup presented by Lady Mary Meynell, so that everyone's contribution was recognised except for unlucky de Laborie who had wrecked his machine. This was the first air meeting to make a profit and a chain was purchased for future Mayoresses of Burton, appropriately with an aircraft incorporated in the design.

Brunneau de Laborie in front of his Farman biplane. This photograph provides an interesting view both of his aircraft and the temporary 'tent' hangar allocated to him. His mechanics are busy in the background, one of them carrying a petrol can of the type used for fuelling the planes.

De Laborie's wrecked machine after his plunge to the ground. Planes carried coloured pennants to help identification. Burton trams and later, buses, also had a coloured route indicator (a light at night) and the Stapenhill colour was green like the pennant on de Laborie's aircraft. A local wit is reputed to have asked de Laborie if he was the aeroplane for Stapenhill but the Frenchman, understandably, appeared nonplussed. After the crash the same wit commented: 'I'm glad I decided to take the tram after all.'

Crowds swarmed to the farm near Lichfield after de Lesseps made his unplanned landing in the Bleriot monoplane. The farmer made a charge for viewing it when it was placed overnight in a barn. All now appears to be ready for the take-off next morning.

The Mayor of Burton, Councillor T. Jenkins, an architect, welcomed de Lesseps back to the airfield when he finally returned from his Lichfield trip, having inadvertently flown on to Nottingham. De Lesseps had covered 41 miles in 30 minutes at an average speed of 80 mph and this was acknowledged as an unofficial record flight, though of course one soon to be beaten. Wetmore gas holder appears in the background.

This is the Mayor about to take a short flight with Beau in the Farman biplane, the structure of its upper wing illustrated here to advantage. Part of Greensmith's mill appears on the right.

Beau was the eventual winner of a trophy for passenger carrying and Mr R.B. Barratt, a coal merchant, holding firmly on behind, was the second local man to ascend, his flight lasting about 3 minutes and reaching a height of 100 feet. This is also a revealing view of the aircraft itself.

Newton Road forms the background for this photograph of Julien Mamet. Houses there provided a grandstand view of the flying, some householders charging for seats at their bedroom windows. This is the Bleriot monoplane and shows well the tail structure. It was out of gratitude for assistance when making his epic Channel flight that Bleriot taught Mamet to fly. His bonny wife stands proudly alongside.

E.L. Scrivens of Doncaster produced photographs of the earlier events there and it is one of his postcards that records this fine portrait of Mlle Helene Dutrieu. She became a popular personality during her visit to Burton and her flying breeches were a much discussed topic. Beau, her passenger here, nonchalantly sits in front of the engine smoking his cigarette.

The sixth competitor was Emile Ladougne, seen in the centre of the picture next to his wife and in front of the Goupy biplane in which he made the longest flight of the week.

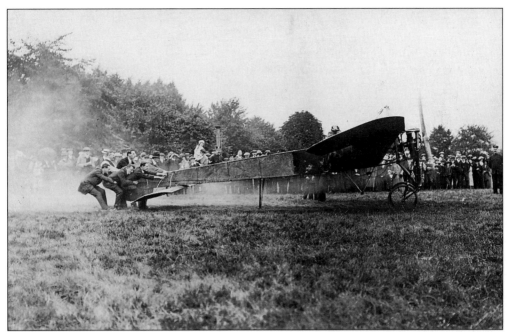

Three other events deserve mention as part of the story of aviation in Burton. On 30 August 1912, H. Salmet, a *Daily Mail* sponsored aviator, visited the town after many delays because of bad weather and was unable to use Bass's Meadow which had flooded. His display had to take place from the Outwoods Recreation Ground. This photograph shows his Bleriot monoplane with helpers holding on to the tail unit - often necessary to restrain these early light machines both before take-off and after landing.

It was back to Bass's Meadow on 1 August 1913 for a third flying meeting featuring Sidney Pickles, an Australian in a Bleriot, and two Englishmen, E. Ronald Whitehouse with a Handley Page monoplane and the Avro biplane in the photograph, piloted by F.P. Raynham. There was a cross country race, circling Repton Church and back, and a 'bombing' display with teacups dropped on the outline of a battleship painted on the grass. Although flying low, no hits were recorded, but 10,000 people enjoyed their day. The Avro illustrates the rapid progress in aeroplane design.

The Burton Corporation gas holder looms in the background and now it is 24 July 1929 and the Mayor, Alderman W.H. Giles, stands alongside the distinguished airman, Sir Alan Cobham, again on Bass's Meadow. Sir Alan had lunched at the Town Hall and parties of councillors await a flight in his air-liner. This followed discussions for an aerodrome at Burton's proposed site off Henhurst Hill, which had been surveyed by Sir Alan and approved by the Air Ministry. It was optimistically proclaimed that the site promised another inducement for local businesses as it practically intersected direct lines from Croydon (then London's airport) to Liverpool and Manchester, Bristol to Hull, and Southampton to Newcastle. The airfield was used for the visit of Cobham's National Aviation Day Display on 11 May 1933 during Burton Civic Week. Cobham's 'Flying Circus' was touring all over the country at this time. The aerodrome project did not advance, however, although the airfield was used by the RAF in the Second World War as No. 16 Elementary Flying School using Puss Moth aeroplanes and was known as RAF Battlestead Hill, also listed as an emergency landing ground. Only the name Aviation Lane survives as a reminder of Burton's proposed local airport, along with the pictorial souvenirs of the town's enthusiastic entry into the exciting new world of aviation in 1910.

Fourteen
Grand Opening Night

A long slow drum roll brought the animated chatter of the large audience to an abrupt end. The house curtain rose for the first time to reveal the Moody Manners Opera Company standing in lines. On either end, in immaculate evening dress, stood William, and his son H.G. Dudley Bennett, the new theatre's proprietors. As the drum roll reached a crescendo the audience rose to its feet to join in singing the *National Anthem*.

The view from the stage of crowded stalls, circle, gallery and balcony, with groups in all the boxes, must have been a satisfying sight for the father and son present on stage for the Grand Opening of their new venture, The Opera House, Burton upon Trent, on that Monday evening 17 November 1902. The curtain now fell again, the orchestra commenced the overture and the gala opening performance of *Faust* was under way.

Between acts three and four a photographer took pictures of the audience from the stage and then between acts four and five the younger Mr Dudley Bennett appeared on stage again to welcome patrons on behalf of his father and himself. The building, formerly St George's Hall, had been extensively rebuilt, extended and completely redesigned over a six month period of intense activity and Mr Dudley Bennett first thanked Corporation officials for their assistance. Their rules and regulations were very stringent but had been met in every possible way. The work of the architects, he felt, fully justified itself and he commended the local building firm of Messrs Lowe & Sons, singling out for mention their foreman, Mr Cotton 'to whose perseverance and energy they owed being able to open on time.' He felt that the decorative work of Messrs Dejong spoke for itself but he expressed a special word of gratitude to the town's own Mr Richards who had installed the electric lighting. It would be the aim of the proprietors, promised Mr Dudley Bennett, 'to study the comfort, convenience and safety of patrons and in return they hoped that the public would give the support which would justify them in offering that excellent entertainment which otherwise they would be unable to provide.' Before bowing he gestured and looked upwards where, high above his head and over the proscenium arch were inscribed the words 'Our True Intent Is All For Your Delight'. The opera then continued and received highly favourable reviews along with opinions that the success of the opening night augured well for the future of this new and much needed centre of entertainment for the town. It was to be an all-too-brief golden age.

Even during the period when the Opera House was being built, 'The Original and Only

Edison's Electric Animated Pictures' was presented in the town. The bioscope, popular at fun fairs, was already being incorporated as part of stage entertainments. Although regarded at first merely as a novelty or diversion (while you went to the bar) many theatres persisted with what was, all too soon, to help bring about their downfall. There were already purpose-built cinemas by 1908; 2,000 halls showed films by 1914. The Burton Opera House began to feature films and cine-variety along with its stage shows in the 1920s and on 21 July 1934, the curtain fell for the last time - and it was across a screen, not a stage set.

The local press commented: 'In its day the Opera House saw many of the world's finest artists; a great number of the most famous plays; and musicians of note delighted patrons with their talents. Viewing James Cagney in *Lady Killer* and John Stuart in *Enemy of the Police* was a unique opportunity of seeing the last of the old theatre preparatory to its conversion into a Wonder Cinema.' Soon the demolition crews moved in to break up and remove the handsome interior that had evoked such enthusiasm just thirty-two years earlier...

'Messrs Bennett's new Opera House will be one of the handsomest theatres in the provinces. The decorating and furnishing throughout are of the French Renaissance design and of the most beautiful and elaborate description; the draperies and upholsteries are in a selected tint of copper colour. The handsome tableau curtain is also richly embroidered in this tint. The act-drop representing Shakespeare's principal characters is a masterpiece of the scene-painter's art, the colours of the decorations and upholstering being cleverly matched in the pictures. The theatre is heated throughout by low pressure hot water pipes and radiators and every care has been taken to preclude draughts and cold air by placing double doors and heavy curtains in all passages and corridors.'

The main entrance was at the side, in George Street, through a lobby lit by 'elaborate electroliers.' One then continued into the crush room where one branched off into the orchestra stalls and thence 'by easy gradients' to the foyer leading to private boxes, dress circle and balcony. There were separate rear entrances to pit and gallery. Prior to opening, the Highways and Sewerage Committee debated the additional provision of external glass awnings to protect anticipated queues and they referred to 'the new Coronation Theatre' - presumably a speculative proposal at the time of Edward VII's accession. This title was not adopted although the Opera House also carried the names New Theatre and Hippodrome, the latter billing used for variety shows.

Once inside ladies might adjourn to the Geisha Room - 'richly upholstered and thickly carpeted in the prevailing tint.' Tea, coffee, ices and other light refreshments were served here during intervals. The name and its theme reflected a current taste for old Japan and China, repeated in many theatrical shows of the period. Burton beers were of course served in the bars and there were 'appropriate retiring rooms for each section of the audience.'

In those first optimistic years of the new century the future for regular, high quality, live, professional entertainment seemed assured, with this gracious building offering, every week, a change of programme, catering for all tastes and prices and, above all, providing that wonderful, friendly, magical atmosphere and escape from everyday life found only in the live theatre. But all over the country the silent films flickered their tempting challenge and when the 'talkies' arrived in 1927, still more theatre audiences deserted. The Opera House was just one of hundreds of theatres which enjoyed a short but memorable golden age as part of the pattern of change in the world of entertainment. Its cinema successor, under various names, has at least ensured that this site remains a centre of entertainment after 130 years. At the rear you can still see much of a facade that was once the front of old St George's Hall of 1867 and there are the bricked-up entrances through which the cheaper seats were reached when the crowds thronged to attend that splendid opening night of the Opera House at the beginning of the new century. It remains a memorial to the drama and comedy, tears and laughter, the lights and the spectacular effects; the warm companionship of fellow spectators and, above all, that indefinable rapport that built up within those walls between audiences and so many great performers of the past.

This interior photograph of the Opera House stage and orchestra pit gives some idea of the drapes and decoration and the quality and size of stage settings. Authors are now asked to use metric measurements so this handsome stage was 10.668 m deep, 13.716 m wide, with a proscenium arch opening of 8.440 m and a height of 9.144 m, with 15.240 m to overhead grids for lowering drop curtains etc. One can only imagine the comments of stage managers if they had consulted the *Stage Year Book* to prepare for their visit to Burton and found that information! Fortunately it told them 35 ft, 45 ft and 28 ft with a height of 30 ft rising to 50 ft in the tower. The 1908 edition would also have given seating capacity as 1,800, which seems very unlikely, even allowing for the old theatrical term 'packing them in' on bench-type gallery seats. The 1912 figure of 1,250 is more realistic and by 1926 it was 950, because with more films now shown, some original seating was no longer usable.

Two performers who had played at Burton, Dolly and Madge McCalla, wrote from the Gaiety Theatre, Birmingham to *The People*, 7 August 1910, about theatrical rhyming slang, including: '"What birches have you to let?" refers to birch brooms and means rooms, while the next question would be "What's the Burton?", this abbreviation for Burton on Trent to be interpreted as rent.'

The audience as seen from the stage on the Grand Opening Night. Almost all those in the dress circle are indeed wearing full evening dress. During a normal week, however, especially on a Monday, many a performer looked out on to 'the Wood family', a theatrical description for rows of empty seats. When this happened, stickers saying 'Big Success - Book Now' would be added to posters round the town to encourage audiences for later in the week.

This view looks into the auditorium, giving a wider impression of the theatre's rich decorative features and drapes and includes part of the overstage inscription.

Simnett's flashlight photograph shows staff and orchestra in the early days of the new theatre, twenty-nine in all. Third from the left is Mr J.W. Wright who had the distinction of serving throughout the theatre's existence, 1902-1934.

Poster-type postcard publicity for *Potash and Perlmutter*, the American play of 1912 which introduced a new kind of broad Jewish dialect humour. It created a theatrical sensation when staged in London in 1914 and was described as 'The Pioneer Wise-Crack Play'. It was the Opera House play on 31 January 1916 when there was a Zeppelin raid on the town, killing fifteen people. Although bombs were falling, most of the audience sang *God Save The King* before leaving.

The Burton Operatic Society and the Burton Amateur Dramatic Club took full advantage of the Opera House and its facilities. This is the cast of the Operatic Society's 1905 production of *The Yeoman of the Guard*. The Society's elaborate Edwardian programmes were very decorative but not to be outdone, the Dramatic Club printed their programme for *The Man From Blankely's* (below, 1911) on silk. In the 1920s, surviving figures show the Operatic Society taking well over £400 during their week at normal theatre prices, allowing them to make a generous donation to charities. The touring company that presented *No, No, Nanette* in 1926 took £739.

After the Opera House closed on 21 July 1934 there was almost total rebuilding except for the wall in George Street, which now became the screen end of the new cinema, the old stage having backed on to Guild Street where the stage doors were. The Ritz was designed in a style typical of new cinemas of the period, as seen here from the balcony.

This 1930s decorative style was carried on into a 'luxurious and well appointed cafe' above the Guild Street entrance and furnished with smart black-top tables and tubular steel chairs. It became a popular rendezvous for morning coffee or for genteel teas before or after the continuous performances. The Ritz, seating 1,500, opened on 11 March 1935 with Richard Tauber in *Blossom Time*.

This has to be the least glamorous of all Opera House photographs. Simnett's own premises closely adjoined the theatre and from his yard he recorded this intriguing view of the stage tower used in raising and lowering scenery, along with various external ladders and walk-ways. Next door to Simnett was Miss Bewick's sweet shop and even here someone has managed to create a garden at least big enough to dry an umbrella.

Burton at the time the Opera House opened in 1902. The water tower on Waterloo Clump, built in 1904, has not yet appeared on the sky line but this once familiar townscape of industrial and brewery premises with their smoking chimneys has almost totally vanished. In the right foreground, however, is the decorative facade of Old St George's Hall. The upper portion has gone but the rest still stands in George Street where the people of Burton queued for the popular seats on the Grand Opening Night of their new theatre.

Fifteen
Recalling
a Unique Tramway

Many pictures record Burton Corporation trams from their first day of operations on 3 August 1903 until the last tram ran from Winshill on 31 December 1929.

The trams that ran between Burton and Ashby have also been extensively recorded. This was a unique service owned by the Midland Railway and operated in competition with its own railway services between Burton, Swadlincote, Newhall, Gresley, Woodville and Ashby. Its twenty open top double deck cars were inscribed Burton and Ashby Light Railways and ran from 2 July 1906 until 19 February 1927.

The most elusive pictures of these trams are those showing them within Burton itself. It is possible that by 1906 photographing trams was less of a novelty, as they were now an accepted feature on town streets. Secondly, the Ashby cars, although working on the Corporation's lines, did not run through the centre of Burton so they never appear on the frequent postcards of High Street or the town end of Station Street. After leaving Wellington Street terminus they used Guild Street and Horninglow Street to reach Trent Bridge and Bearwood Hill before leaving High Bank Road to continue their 'switchback' route to Ashby, 10.2 miles taking 80 minutes and, until 1919, costing 6d ($2\frac{1}{2}$p). A direct Midland train from Burton took about 20 minutes.

This story has to begin, however, at Swadlincote where the system was based with the depot and workshops. Here 3-cylinder diesel engines and a Westinghouse generator provided electric power and battery charging. The first tram delivered was carried by the Midland Railway from the brush works at Loughborough and appears here being unloaded in Swadlincote goods yard minus top deck fitting and bogie.

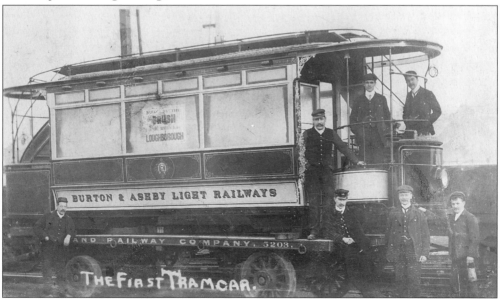

Car 10 from Ashby heads for Wellington Street with Station Street looking very slushy and dirty, *c.* 1910. Ashby trams can be recognised through having the destination board above the driver (Burton trams above the upper deck) and the staircase to the driver's left. Above the shops (left) at this time was the Bridge Temperance Hotel and the premises below included those of local photographers Horace Dudley and Ernest Abrahams. Both seem to have ignored the trams passing their doors.

A rare view of an Ashby tram in Guild Street. Car 8 appears to be empty with the crew having trouble with the trolley pole. These trams were painted in Midland Railway crimson-lake, with off-white top deck decency boards and lower deck rocker panels lined in gold leaf with ornate decorative corners. All the background in this scene has now been swept away, including Bass stores and maltings.

A busy scene at the junction of Guild Street with Horninglow Street, near the entrance to the Corporation tram depot but actually capturing two Ashby cars together at a passing point before the single track Guild Street section. An intrepid motorist has decided to overtake. The domed court house ('It might be a variety theatre' - Pevsner) opened in 1910. The original office of the old Town Commissioners still occupies Guild Street corner. It became the transport offices but a drab new block later replaced this pleasant Victorian building. Note also the brewery 'floater' cart.

After crossing Trent Bridge and ascending Bearwood Hill (where tram 19 ran back and overturned on 8 October 1919), Ashby trams turned into High Bank Road where Burton Corporation built nearly a mile of track to the Borough boundary for the new service. Here a car for Burton sweeps down through the open country that still surrounded old Winshill. A lost landmark from these early years of the century is the chimney stacks of Hodges' brick works, situated off the 'level' on Bearwood Hill Road.

This view looking up Bearwood Hill shows work in progress during the widening of Trent Bridge in 1926. Following the derailment of 1919 the tram lines were given a more direct approach to the gradient but it was a belated move as all tram services soon ended. With increasing motor traffic and the problems of crossing Newton Road, this particular layout was short lived. Many people probably feel that not all traffic difficulties have yet been satisfactorily resolved here.

You could still spot tram No. 14 today operating at the World Free Trade Centre in Detroit, USA. This original photograph shows it near Gresley Common with driver Charles Wells and conductor Leonard James. It would be splendid if this unique tram, rescued and largely restored in South Derbyshire, could be returned to its territory. Reflecting on some causes benefiting from National Lottery funds, one wonders if No. 14 might not be brought home to a purpose-built museum with its own length of track as an additional tourist attraction - perhaps through a part of the new National Forest.

Sixteen

In Lighter Vein

A good looking Welsh tourist has lately been "doing" this Country and has made the following notes with reference to Kissing in different parts. He found that the **Bilston** girls keep quite still until they are well kissed, and then say, " I think you ought to be ashamed of yourself " A **Brierley Hill** girl when kissed closes her eyes in ecstacy, and does not open them again until she is sure there is no more. A **Burslem** girl on being kissed says "Oh" very softly, for fear some one should come and stop it. A marriageable maiden of **Burton-on-Trent** on being kissed, tries to look stern, fails, then slides her little hand into that of the bold, bad man, and in a voice as soft as Blanc Mange, whispers ten⁻derly, "Oh, George, what are your intentions ? The girls of **Cannock** say, " Well, I never thought it of you, and I am very much surprised and I hope you won't try to do it again, but don't let us stop here where it is light ; let us go out of the town where no one will see us.

LOVERS LANE . **Branstone Road, BURTON.**
MY WORD, IF YOU'RE NOT OFF !   "Scott" Series C84

These are typical light-hearted sentimental postcards of the period prior to the First World War. We hardly feel qualified to comment on the first item (from an Edwardian postcard, *Kissing in Staffordshire*), while Branstone Road seems an unlikely choice as a Lovers Lane, but of course both are a standard design adapted to suit any locality. Both belong to the time when 'billing and cooing', 'canoodling' and 'spooning' were the 'in' words to describe romantic episodes. The cartoon policemen are an anachronism anyway for Staffordshire, where the force was equipped with flat pill-box type caps.

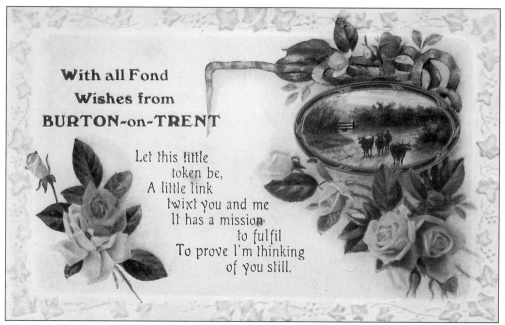

Again a standard design, but this particular example could equally well be used for a birthday, for Christmas or even as a valentine. This one has been sent with Christmas greetings and many Edwardian Christmas cards were, in fact, of postcard type - a penny postcard, a halfpenny stamp and no need for an envelope! Posted early on Christmas Day itself it would be in time for a local Christmas Day delivery.

An Allsopps Lager advertising card, c. 1903/4, making use of the latest novelty - the motor car. 'The hand' refers, of course, to the symbol on the Allsopps bottle. This red hand trade mark, dating back to the 1850s, caused some problems, including design changes in the positions of fingers and thumb, in one instance to obviate suggestions of vulgarity. This is a good early example of the use of a cartoon for advertising purposes.

100

Seventeen

War and Peace

The outbreak of the First World War on 4 August 1914 led to considerable military activity in the town. Local photographs now reflected the new circumstances and often featured locations seldom pictured before, making them doubly interesting today. This example, with a unit marching towards Moor Street bridge, shows old cottages with little front gardens that stood left of the Forest Gate Inn; Christ Church still, of course, with its spire; Briggs' Engineering works (right); and behind the hoarding, the goods depot of the London and North Western Railway. On the farther side of it there was only a footpath leading to Anglesey Road with no direct road connection until the late 1920s. From Dale Street the subsequent line of Anglesey Road ran past Briggs', served Sykes' Brewery and the Crown Maltings and was called Sykes Street on the ordnance map of 1884, becoming Kimmersitch Street (recalling an ancient name) and finally Anglesey Road. Note the typical Burton railway sleeper fence on the right.

The Crown maltings appear here as background to a parade of 6th Battalion North Staffs recruits, along with a rare view of Dale Street signal box on the Midland Railway's Bond End and Shobnall branch line. Like most other town boxes there is the warning bell which heralded the closing of the gates. Burton pedestrians became adept at breaking into a canter in order to beat trains across the town's many level crossings of which, at one time, there were over thirty.

As well as companies of the 6th Battalion North Staffs, Burton's Territorial forces included 'C' squadron of the Staffordshire Yeomanry and members of this force are assembled here near the Peter Walker Brewery in Clarence Street. Many brewery horses and wagons were commandeered in the early days of the war. With over 1,000 reservists billeted in Peach's maltings there was an urgent need for baggage transport. Peach's maltings later housed German prisoners of war when building the wall round Branston depot.

C. Sq: Staff: Yeomanry Cookhouse at Frenze.

Burton photographer Ernest Abrahams produced many fine local views and studio portraits but he also contributed a valuable collection of military scenes, including many aspects of the wartime activities of the Staffordshire Yeomanry. He was with them while they were stationed at Frenze, near Diss in Norfolk, and some of his photographs are equally of social history interest, for example, his informal study of an army cookhouse in those blissful days when we had never heard of E coli or BSE.

Members of the Burton branch of the Red Cross Society went quickly into action when war broke out. Within four days the Town Hall had become a Red Cross hospital with Miss Mary Thompson (third from left, front row) as Commandant. In 1918 she was awarded the OBE for her services. We would be interested to know the location for this photograph; it would seem to be a barn with a high entrance for loaded wagons.

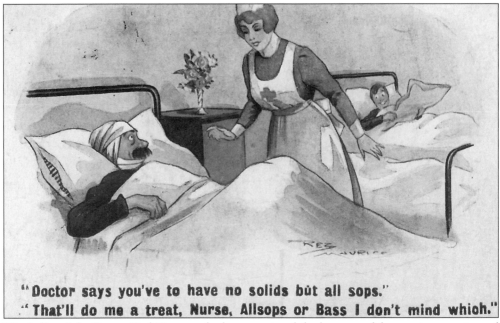

"Doctor says you've to have no solids but all sops."
"That'll do me a treat, Nurse, Allsops or Bass I don't mind which."

The ladies of the Burton Red Cross no doubt appreciated the humour of the wartime comic card with its local 'flavour'. The Town Hall hospital was quickly in use, with Belgian soldiers among its first patients. An additional ward was established in St Paul's Institute. Both were mainly staffed by local VAD (Voluntary Aid Detachments) members.

Burton Daily Mail

THE LARGEST LOCAL PAPER WITH THE LARGEST SALE.

No. 5,620   CHRISTMAS 1916   ONE HALF-PENNY

From the Readers of the " Burton Daily Mail" wishing you a Jolly Christmas and the best of Luck in the New Year.

"BURTON—TO BURTON BOYS, GREETING."

AGAIN we share our Christmas fare
  With our lads who are far away,
Fighting the foe in the trenches low,
  And daring the deadly fray.

We have taken care of our lads out there,
  But our hearts are warm: And wide
We our purses ope to their furthest scope
  For our other lads beside.

There are those of the band who guard our
  land,
  And the lads in the hospital blue,
There are them just gone from the warm
  hearthstone
  To the training so strange and new,

And to all and to each we fain would reach
  With our gift this Christmas-tide;
While we pray that the Year which now
   draws near,
  May see each at his own fireside!

May Strife soon cease, and a lasting Peace
  Our banners victorious crown;
And old Burton's sons who have manned the
  guns
  Come back to old Burton town!
           NINA SERETTE.

Burton-on-Trent,
  December, 1916.

For Christmas 1916 a *Burton Daily Mail* postcard sent greetings to those serving in the British Expeditionary Force along with a supply of Christmas puddings. On the reverse of Nina Serette's sentimental piece was a more light-hearted poem by 'T.A.D.' addressed to 'Burton boys on service in Great Britain' and advising them to eat their puddings promptly in the face of threatened additional restrictions, prohibitions and officious food controllers! Sugar was the first food to be rationed in 1917.

Burton Patriotic Fair in June 1917 developed from three ladies - Mrs Adams, Mrs Fitchett and Mrs Mason - proposing a modest garden party in aid of war charities. The project became the biggest local gala occasion since the Coronation of King George V in 1911 and was held in Stapenhill Recreation Grounds and in Councillor W.P. Stanley's meadow (Stapenhill Hollow was not then part of the Recreation Grounds). It was opened by Lady Noreen Bass and raised over £2,000. This scene shows the Allies Flower Stall, part of the Ladies' Market, with each municipal ward organising a stand.

The Patriotic Fair attractions included five concert parties, orchestras, a male voice choir, the Nottinghamshire Regimental Band, dancing, sports and, on the river, swimming, diving and boat races. War trophies were displayed, among them relics of a Zeppelin brought down at Potters Bar. The Festival Theatre was erected near the Spring Terrace Road entrance. A fancy dress parade by wounded soldiers, shown here, reflected the wide range of the allied forces, now including the Americans who entered the war on 5 April 1917. It was a spectacular event to brighten the dark days of the third year of the conflict.

Peace Celebrations marking the end of the First World War were staged nationally and locally on Saturday 19 July 1919 (eight months after hostilities ended). A Burton procession lined up in the Grange Field and progressed via the Town Hall, Station Street, High Street, Lichfield Street and Branston Road to the National Machine Gun Factory (Branston Depot) where lunch was served in two sittings for ex-servicemen. A grand free gala followed on the Ox-hay, ending with fireworks. Members of the Corporation travelled in this stately vehicle, seen passing the corner of Union Street and Station Street, the vantage point for the following scenes.

Some demobilised soldiers carried this banner but contemporary accounts merely commented that it 'puzzled many people.' It was plainly a private joke. The design shows a fish and a tankard with '2' on it. At 111 New Street once stood the Fish and Quart (2 pints!). Around this time it closed and, with adjoining properties, was later demolished for infirmary extensions. Was this a play on words for a favourite pub's last 'draught' with 'Eff and Kue' representing the initials of Fish and Quart?

Typical motor vehicles of the period are seen to advantage here, while an interesting fashion note is that every single person in view wears headgear of some kind. In the front car are Colonel John Gretton MP and the Hon Mrs Gretton. Other prominent local figures were in the following vehicles. For the victorious military, of course, it was another route march for their free lunch, then back again to the Ox-hay for the gala. One suspects that some of them adjourned to local hostelries for private reunions.

The Red Cross, Girl Guides and Women's Voluntary Services were all represented in the procession but this scene is of current interest in providing a record of many well known Burton shops only very recently swept away be redevelopment. Familiar names that traded at different times between Union Street Corner and Bass's New Brewery included Emerys; Sherratt, florist; Heape and Wibberley and Phillips & Co., both house furnishers; Hunter's Stores (for a short time a branch of Boots) and Shelleys, estate agents.

Burton War Memorial was not unveiled until August 1922. On 11 November 1919 and again in 1920, an Armistice Day service was held in the Parish Church. In 1921, however, a temporary cenotaph was erected in the Market Place and a hugh crowd attended an outdoor service. This scarce photograph by Ernest Abrahams depicts the memorial after the ceremony but we can find no record of what happened to it. Eighteen years later the country was again at war.

After the war a tank was presented to the town at a ceremony in King Edward Place. As well as the number 286 it carried an unofficial inscription: 'Daisy the Maneater', and the name *Burtonia* was also added. It was then placed on display at the approach to Trent Bridge, near where public toilets were built, until the widening of the bridge in 1924-6. This scene, taken during the widening, looks towards the area where Wetmore Bus Park was established and *Burtonia* can be seen on the extreme left with Trent House behind.

Eighteen

Tales from the Riverbank

The name Burton upon Trent not only distinguishes the town from over thirty other Burtons but emphasises the significance of the river to the town. There is evidence of very early settlement of the Trent valley in the vicinity, even if the first occupation of the site of Burton itself remains obscure. The Romans recorded the river as Trisantona, an old British name which Ekwall suggests means 'trespasser' because of its frequent flooding. It became Treanta or Treenta in Saxon times and Trenta by the time of Domesday. Curving around for some 170 miles from near Biddulph Moor until it enters the Humber, it inevitably became both a route for invading peoples and new settlers as well as a navigable waterway for the development of trade. Broadholme and Horseholm are reminders of Danish invaders, whose word 'holm' for an island gave us these names. The Trent also became the natural boundary between tribal areas and later the counties. Settlements grew up where there were fords or easy crossing places and early inhabitants benefited from the fish and wild fowl readily available, while the river was once famed for its salmon. It was on the banks of the Trent that Burton developed, the river playing a vital part in the town's long history. The scene shows the Trent valley south of Burton with the Leicester line bridge and viaduct but no Drakelow power station to dominate the sky-line.

Before the big post-war housing developments Waterside was a favourite venue for boating expeditions, perhaps with a picnic on the bank, or calling off to visit friends at one of the many little riverside bungalows used as weekend retreats, often complete with moorings or boathouse. For rowers and walkers the Gardens Hotel was available for light refreshment and it was indeed noted for its fine garden in which entertainments, strawberry teas and dances were once very popular. A few bungalows remain today below the Leicester line bridge.

For the more energetic users of the river another favourite rendezvous was the White Swan at Walton, and many people rowed up past Drakelowe Hall to enjoy a drink or a picnic. One such occasion, catered for on quite a big scale, was this Leander Rowing Club gathering shortly before the First World War. Although there is a teapot on one table, everyone seems to have chosen an alternative.

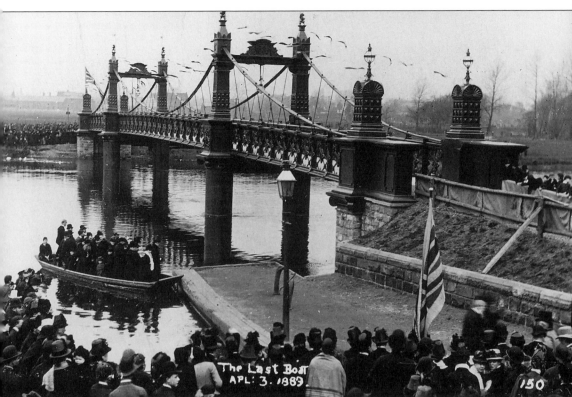

The Last Boat
APL: 3. 1889.

150

On Wednesday 3 April 1889 the Ferry Bridge, Lord Burton's gift to the town, was declared open by Lady Burton and the ancient Stapenhill ferry operated for the last time. This scene shows the decorated bridge and crowds assembled for the ceremony. From early morning full boatloads were ferried across as people took a last trip. If this caption is correct, it is ten minutes to ten because the order was then given to cease ferry traffic. The boat was, however, to make one more journey. To rousing cheers, Lord Burton and his party who had driven from Rangemore to Stapenhill House, residence of C.J. Clay JP, now walked down Jerram's Lane and boarded the ferry boat. Lady Burton entered first, followed by Lord Burton, Sir W. and Lady Plowden, the Hon Miss Bass, the Mayor and Mrs Harrison, the Misses Thornewill, Mr and Mrs C.J. Clay and Mr G. Burton. Safely across, they went up on to the bridge for the formalities. The Mayor presented Lady Burton with a boatshaped fruit dish in solid silver, its engravings including a representation of the bridge and an appropriate inscription. The work was carried out by Mr A.J. Wright, jeweller of 170 High Street. Lord Burton was then given an elaborate illuminated address subscribed for by over 5,000 people. Sir W. Plowden MP replied on behalf of Lord Burton who had a throat infection and the official party then adjourned to St Paul's Institute for one of those occasions beloved by the Victorians - a banquet with innumerable courses, toasts and interminable speeches. The public cheerfully crossed and re-crossed the bridge and no doubt drank in local hostelries to the words on a banner draped across The Dingle - 'Three Cheers For Bass'.

J.L. 'Jimmy' Greensmith (left) examines a typical flat bottomed sailing boat washed down the river from Drakelow Deeps during one of the annual floods, and stranded on the weir near Greensmith's Mill at Winshill. The mill can be seen through the trees.

A conventional Trent Bridge view, but recording the rowing club scene. From the left, along the bank, are the clubhouses of Trent (1863), Leander (1847) and Burton Rowing Club (1863). Burton Regatta was jointly established in 1865 but there were social differences in the memberships, Trent RC being mainly manual workers. Because of supposed physical advantages, there was controversy between national rowing bodies which spilled over locally. Burton RC eventually amalgamated to form Burton Leander RC and they and Trent RC now flourish competitively. Note the water sheds into which boats were backed for storage. When clinker-built, they were heavy to lift and leaked if dried out.

This scene was snapped just before the First World War alongside the Leicester line railway bridge and shows 'one of the junior events at the local regatta. Dick is stroke in the boat nearest the camera. They have just won a final and are backing into the boathouse.' The bridge, built by the Midland Railway, dates from 1849 and this view shows the Derbyshire side of it, the finishing line when the regatta course was over the Drakelow Deeps.

A fine array of trophies on display as preparations are completed for the prize distribution ceremony after another successful regatta. The Mayor (1920-21), A.H. Yeomans, is second from the right. The flat caps (left) are worn by members of Worthingtons band who played during the afternoon.

THE ORDER

In which Boats will be placed in the PROCES-
SION, on Wednesday, June 24th, according to the
Ballot, at the Leander Club House.

No.	Names of Boats.	Owners.
1	Leander,	Leander Boat Club
2	Titania,	Mr. Warham
3	Water Witch,	Mr. J. Cartwright
4	Undine,	Mr. Drewry
5	Dodo,	Leander Boat Club
6	Alliance.	Mr. Forman's Band
7	L'Hirondelle,	Mr. F. Tompson
8	Daisy,	Mr. A. Bass
9	Lily,	Mr. J. Thornewill
10	Prosperous	Mr. E. Cliff
11	Constance,	Mr. Jackson
12	Blue Jacket,	Mr. Downing
13	Flora,	Mr. G. Nadin
14	Rover,	Mr. E. Cliff
15	Queen,	Leander Boat Club
16	Martha,	Mr. E. Cliff
17	Helen,	Mr. Joseph Nadin
18	Firefly,	Mr. R. Thornewill
19	Empress,	Mr. J. Cartwright
20	Alma,	Mr. Ratcliff
21	Mary,	Rev. S. Stead
22	Hebe,	Mr. Phillips
23	Hippopotamus	Mr. Salt
24	Frolic,	Leander Boat Club
25	Sylph,	Mr. T. Robinson
26	Modwena,	Mr. R. Thornewill
27	Blink Bonny,	Mr. E. Cliff
28	Eugenie,	Mr. Forman
29	Hesperus,	Mr. Brown
30	Mystery,	Mr. Goodger

(35) June 23 J. W. LEES, COMMODORE.

A surviving printer's proof copy recalls a very early example of an organised event on the river. Ten years after their formation and before the first regatta, Leander Club arranged this boat procession for 24 June 1857. Some well known family names from mid-Victorian Burton are listed among boat owners. The pencil marks are probably amended entries for the following year but it is interesting to note a steam yacht added at the top.

C.J.S. ORION.
BURTON WATER CARNIVAL 1910.

In 1910 a water carnival was staged as a finale to the flower show. Decorated and illuminated boats covered a circular course with an Operatic Society choir singing appropriate songs in the leading boat, and there was a firework display to complete the occasion. One elaborate entry was from Mr C.J. Spooner, of fairground fame, who converted his boat into a miniature replica of the Dreadnought *Orion*.

114

Later river carnivals were staged during Burton Shopping Week, September/October 1931, and as part of Civic Week celebrations in May 1933. Swans were an obvious choice for the decorated boat processions but the 1933 winning entry was, in fact, disguised as a peacock. That year an estimated 30,000 people lined the riverbanks, the carnival ending with a 'spectacular firework display' on the Broadholme. Tickets for the illuminated Stapenhill Recreation Ground cost 6d ($2\frac{1}{2}$p) with one proviso: 'Perambulators will not be admitted to the grounds'.

There were contrasting scenes along the banks of that arm of the river passing by Wetmore. This postcard photograph was taken during Aviation Week, 1910, and includes the frail structure of the aircraft's wings. It shows Wetmore Road and the gas works with the town in a haze of smoke from industrial and domestic chimneys. Also of interest here is the Saturday night postmark, Burton 10.45 pm with a message to Luton: 'Shall be back today, Sunday, about 10.30 am.' Late night posting for early next day delivery, including Sunday, was then normal service for the cost of a halfpenny stamp.

This is an interesting photograph in that it records comparatively recent changes to the river-banks. Alligator Point was where two arms of the river combined, the right hand one in this scene being the popular open air swimming area with the old bathing sheds situated to the extreme right on the Ox-hay. Although this arm was subsequently filled in, its course can still be traced, but Alligator Point is no longer a distinctive feature.

We mentioned the old name for the Trent meaning 'the trespasser'. This photograph contrasts the quiet river of earlier pictures with a flood scene. This is the Bridge Street end of Trent Bridge looking towards Wetmore, with the river over its banks and the Hay sidings awash. Left, is the former Nunnerley Brewery and beyond, is Trent House. Note the roof of the gallery built by surgeon and naturalist R.B. Mason for his collection of 13,000 zoological and botanical specimens, many acquired along the riverbanks that have been the subject of this group of scenes.

Nineteen

Days to Remember

By the turn of the century improved transport facilities allowed many better off families to enjoy a traditional seaside holiday but for the great majority, before the time of holidays with pay, a day's outing or even a half-day trip, perhaps once or twice in the year, could be a memorable occasion. For many children Sunday School outings were a special treat, while a lot of organisations and groups arranged some kind of visit for their members. When so many people stayed at home, fêtes and galas were treated very much as holiday outings. When trips were arranged, favourite local spots were Tutbury Castle and the grounds of Rolleston Hall, Bretby Park and Brizlincote Hall. Further afield but with easy and fairly inexpensive transport, Ashby Castle and Dovedale were popular. Burton of course, was known nationally for the celebrated Bass trips, among the largest company excursions ever run. Our selection of 'Days To Remember' looks at some less spectacular occasions which still remained in people's memories long afterwards, aided by the souvenir photographs recalling these happy days out.

Not to overlook the Bass trips, however, this view of the Britannia Pier at Yarmouth prompted the following paragraph in the booklet for 1909 when Yarmouth was the resort visited: 'At the entrance to the pier will be found... the helter skelter which affords endless fun to thousands of visitors - this structure was made by our respected townsman, Mr C.J. Spooner of the Trent Bridge works, and was, I understand, completed and erected in a short time from the date of the order.' It had a canvas cover which flapped very merrily in the east coast sea breezes.

A scene at one of Burton's many gala occasions where an ever-popular attraction was a display by Burton Ladies' Fire Brigade. Members would demonstrate jumping into a net from a tall canvas structure. They would then be driven at speed across the riverside meadows and the tower would be set alight so that they could operate hoses and carry out a 'rescue'. These lively ladies provided good entertainment but it was to be many decades before women became involved in real fire fighting.

Bretby Hall, belonging to the Earl of Carnarvon, and Brizlincote Hall were both conveniently served by tramcars of the Burton and Ashby Light Railways. These heavily loaded cars are setting off from outside Holy Trinity Church, Church Gresley, (now demolished) for a Sunday School treat at Brizlincote in August 1910. On such occasions there seems to have been a total disregard for official loading capacity and there were claims of crews competing to see how many they could convey on 'their' tram.

After various uses since closure, the Wesleyan Chapel in Ferry Street, Stapenhill, has now become rehearsal rooms for the Operatic Society. These scenes, our informant tells us, belong to its heyday 'around the time of the First World War.' The costumes perhaps suggest just after rather than before, but for a small Sunday School group like this, a horse drawn wagonette was still the favoured transport for a local visit.

Chamber of Trade.
Picnic to Dovedale. June 26/12.

Half day closing was, of necessity, the time chosen for traders to have an annual outing. There was no question of arranging a Sunday trip in those days! Burton's half day used to be Wednesday and on 26 June 1912, Chamber of Trade members left by the 1.40 pm train of the North Staffordshire Railway to visit Dovedale. It appears to be quite a formal dress occasion with probably little more than a gentle stroll into the dale before adjourning to the Peveril of the Peak hotel for a picnic and a photograph. Ernest Abrahams, the photographer, was no doubt one of the party and so able to combine business with pleasure.

One Burton Archaeological Society outing of 1909 was to Rolleston Hall, where the house, museum and grounds were inspected under the personal guidance of Sir Oswald Mosley, who also entertained the company to lunch. Afterwards the Hon L.F. Tyrwhitt, Rector of Rolleston, gave members a talk at the church before the party moved on to Craythorne where Mr R. Thornewill and his wife welcomed members to tea. Perhaps the generous provision of refreshments encouraged the attendance of sixty-five, the average for the four outings that year being thirty-five!

Burton station was a favourite place for a photograph before setting out by train. On 22 August 1931, Worthington's coopers set off for Belle Vue, Manchester, long a popular venue for railway excursions. In 1859 a trip went from Derby and Egginton, fare 4s (20p) including admission, and with the assurance that one travelled in closed carriages. Belle Vue was established in 1836 but today housing estates cover most of the old grounds which, for over a hundred years, made it the Alton Towers of its time.

Once again Wednesday half day closing was chosen for the local newsagents' outing to Blackpool in 1928, getting away after the completion of the morning paper deliveries. Station notice boards here are a reminder that the LNER (previously the Great Northern Railway) ran into Burton from Nottingham and Lincoln, which also facilitated trips to the east coast resorts like Mablethorpe and Skegness. Worthy of comment is the array of hats worn by the ladies and youngsters alike, all typical of the cloche style fashionable at this time.

Swadlincote shop assistants in very smart attire for their visit to the Bass Brewery. The background helps to make this a splendid picture, with the rows of maltings (now all gone) and the Bass visitors' carriage being hauled by one of the company's locomotives over their own lines *en route* for the ale stores at Shobnall. It is almost certainly locomotive No. 9 in charge and this engine and coach are now displayed at the Bass Museum.

For many people one of the year's highlights was the local flower show, each district of the town staging its own event, often on a large scale. The Morgans, who lived in a canal-side cottage at Shobnall near the Mount Pleasant inn (all swept away) were highly successful with their floral entries at the Horninglow and Shobnall shows of 1910. Here George Morgan, a brewery foreman, and his wife Linda display their prize blooms and winner certificates.

An appropriate inclusion in this section shows horse drawn brakes of George Wellings, cab proprietor, outside 263 Shobnall Street, in 1908. These were used for many a local outing. T.H. Wellings also operated from 84 Sydney Street. Subsequently, as motor vehicles superseded horse transport, George Wellings moved to 55 Derby Street where Mrs Miller had operated a cab business, and established his garage and coach hire service. This postcard photograph advises Mr Chawner, an Anslow farmer, that the chestnut horse is now available for sale.

This was surely a day to remember for some at least of these young people from around Woodville who posed together for this artistically grouped photograph by Joseph Perks - especially as there were two girls present for every male! It is a scene which completely captures the charm, dignity and serenity so often associated with gracious Edwardian summer afternoons.

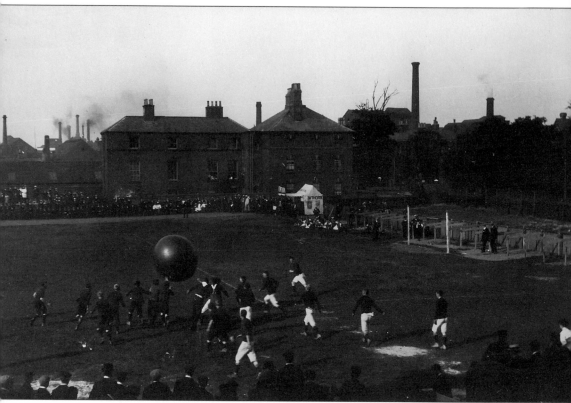

For those attending this Burton event it would be a day to remember because of the unusual nature of the sport they are watching. The game of push ball was introduced into Britain in 1902 and played at the Crystal Palace, London. The *Daily Mail* sponsored some push ball events but it never became popular. The ball used was 6 ft in diameter and weighed 50 lbs. If it was pushed under the goal bar five points were scored; throwing it over the bar counted for eight points. In this game at Peel Croft there appears to be no bar so presumably those standing by the goal are judges. This scene is also an interesting local view. Peel House stands in the centre but all other background features have disappeared including, of course, the Lichfield Street tram standards. The tall chimney to the right of Peel House marks Charrington's Brewery, now the site of the B & Q store.

Twenty

At War Again

The year 1939 saw the outbreak of the Second World War, confirmed in a memorable broadcast to the nation by the Prime Minister, Neville Chamberlain, on Sunday 3 September at 11.00 am. Unlike the First World War it immediately affected everyone in the town. Irrespective of calls for the military, other essential services or war work, the development of air power meant that even the civilian population was, potentially, in the front line. An Air Raid Precautions (ARP) Committee had been formed in 1936; the enrolment of volunteers for civil defence began in 1938 against a threatening international background. The original ARP Committee became the Emergency Committee to co-ordinate every aspect of the home front from civil defence to food rationing. The Corporation produced a *Citizens' Handbook* of wartime information and advice. Although by 1942 it had assumed quite large proportions, we have a small, incomplete early draft copy with provisional typewritten slips gummed below neat little drawings, as in Duties of the Citizen. Various sections covered householders and shopkeepers, road users, police, fire fighters, the Home Guard, first aid workers, gas masks, fire watching duties, food production and the voluntary services.

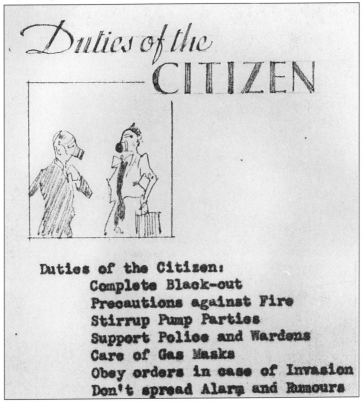

Duties of the Citizen:
Complete Black-out
Precautions against Fire
Stirrup Pump Parties
Support Police and Wardens
Care of Gas Masks
Obey orders in case of Invasion
Don't spread Alarm and Rumours

On 14 May 1940 the formation of a new defence force, the Local Defence Volunteers was announced. At the suggestion of Mr Winston Churchill, the LDV became the Home Guard on 23 July and on 4 August, the new Burton and District Group was reviewed on the Bass Meadows by the Lord Lieutenant of Staffordshire, the Earl of Harrowby. After a series of demonstrations the company paraded in front of the pavilion. Already, nation wide, 1,300,000 volunteers had joined the Home Guard though, as seen here, not all were yet in possession of a weapon.

An additional wartime measure with the limitations and other difficulties over travel, was the provision for holidays at home. In 1943 the arm of the river alongside the Ox-hay was cleared and tidied and clean gravel was put down to create Burton's home-holiday setting.

Among Second World War military visitors to Burton were considerable numbers of American soldiers during the period before D-day. Many of them were billeted in maltings off Wetmore Road, leading to such unexpected scenes as this photograph of an American shunting locomotive operating amongst brewery buildings.

Another temporary wartime expedient was the location of the American Army Post Office in upstairs premises at the Abbey Arcade, revealed here in this rare photograph. Even if it is an exercise bike one can hardly imagine that any form of cycling ever took place in the town's own dignified New Street Post Office. But then a great many things changed after 1939!

We end these brief memories of the Second World War by recalling the relief and thankfulness for final victory with VJ Day on 15 August 1945. Street parties and other events were quickly arranged, though without many men and women still in the forces. This is the Mill Hill Lane (Winshill) victory party. Among the residents are Edith Ward, Len Everett and Gladys Marjoram (standing, extreme left). The Corporation bus FA 7872 was a Guy Arab vehicle supplied in 1940-41 and withdrawn in 1950. In a small way they too marked the end of an era - they were the last local buses to carry route colour light indicators.

Acknowledgements

Apart from the known and unknown photographers who have made this book possible, we are indebted to the following for help in providing additional identification and information: Mrs Olive Hudson (née Farrington), Messrs Eric Fower, Joe Marston, Alan Meikle, Robert Meikle, Alf Moss, Ben Ward and Michael Young.

We also acknowledge assistance from Burton upon Trent Public Library and from the files of the *Burton Mail*.

Finally, our thanks to Miss Michelle Farman, a young lady whose techniques go beyond carbon paper and typewriter for preparing our text for publication.

We always welcome hearing from readers who can correct or add to our archive records.